Functional Programming in R 4

Advanced Statistical Programming for Data Science, Analysis, and Finance

Second Edition

Thomas Mailund

apress®

Functional Programming in R 4: Advanced Statistical Programming for Data Science, Analysis, and Finance

Thomas Mailund
Aarhus N, Denmark

ISBN-13 (pbk): 978-1-4842-9486-4   ISBN-13 (electronic): 978-1-4842-9487-1
https://doi.org/10.1007/978-1-4842-9487-1

Managing Director, Apress Media LLC: Welmoed Spahr
Acquisitions Editor: Melissa Duffy
Development Editor: James Markham
Editorial Project Manager: Mark Powers

Cover designed by eStudioCalamar

Cover image by Max van den Oetelaar on Unsplash (www.unsplash.com)

Distributed to the book trade worldwide by Apress Media, LLC, 1 New York Plaza, New York, NY 10004, U.S.A. Phone 1-800-SPRINGER, fax (201) 348-4505, e-mail orders-ny@springer-sbm.com, or visit www.springeronline.com. Apress Media, LLC is a California LLC and the sole member (owner) is Springer Science + Business Media Finance Inc (SSBM Finance Inc). SSBM Finance Inc is a **Delaware** corporation.

For information on translations, please e-mail booktranslations@springernature.com; for reprint, paperback, or audio rights, please e-mail bookpermissions@springernature.com.

Apress titles may be purchased in bulk for academic, corporate, or promotional use. eBook versions and licenses are also available for most titles. For more information, reference our Print and eBook Bulk Sales web page at http://www.apress.com/bulk-sales.

Any source code or other supplementary material referenced by the author in this book is available to readers on GitHub (https://github.com/Apress). For more detailed information, please visit http://www.apress.com/source-code.

Printed on acid-free paper

Table of Contents

About the Author

Thomas Mailund is Senior Software Architect at Kvantify, a quantum computing company from Denmark. He has a background in math and computer science. He now works on developing algorithms for computational problems applicable for quantum computing. He previously worked at the Bioinformatics Research Centre, Aarhus University, on genetics and evolutionary studies, particularly comparative genomics, speciation, and gene flow between emerging species. He has published *Beginning Data Science in R* with Apress, as well as other books out there.

About the Technical Reviewer

Megan J. Hirni is currently pursuing her PhD at the University of Missouri-Columbia with a focus on applied statistics research. In addition to her love for R coding, Megan loves meeting new people and learning new topics in multifaceted fields.

Acknowledgments

I would like to thank Duncan Murdoch and the people on the R-help mailing list for helping me work out a kink in lazy evaluation in the trampoline example.

CHAPTER 1

Introduction

Welcome to *Functional Programming in R 4*. I wrote this book to have teaching material beyond the typical introductory level most textbooks on R have, where functions are simple constructions for wrapping up some reusable instructions that you can then call when you need those instructions run. In languages such as R, functions are more than this. They are objects in their own right that you can also treat as data, create and manipulate and pass around like other objects, and learning how to do this will make you a far more effective R programmer.

The R language is a multiparadigm language with elements from procedural programming, object-oriented programming, and functional programming. Procedural programming focuses on the instructions you want the computer to execute—add these numbers, put the result in this variable, loop through this list, etc. Object-oriented programming, on the other hand, focuses on what kind of data you manipulate, which operations you can perform on them, and how they change when you manipulate them. If you are interested in these aspects of the R language, I have written another book, *Advanced Object-Oriented Programming in R*, also by Apress, that you might be interested in.

Functional programming is the third style of programming, where the focus is on transformations. Functions transform data from input to output, and by composing transformations, you construct programs from simpler functions to more involved pipelines for your data. In functional programming, functions themselves are considered data, and just as with other data, you can write transformations that take functions as input and

© Thomas Mailund 2023
T. Mailund, *Functional Programming in R 4*, https://doi.org/10.1007/978-1-4842-9487-1_1

produce (other) functions as output. You can thus write simple functions, then adapt them (using other functions to modify them), and combine them in various ways to construct complete programs.

The R programming language supports procedural programming, object-oriented programming, and functional programming, but it is mainly a functional language. It is not a "pure" functional language. Pure functional languages will not allow you to modify the state of the program by changing values parameters hold and will not allow functions to have side effects (and need various tricks to deal with program input and output because of it).

R is somewhat close to "pure" functional languages. In general, data is immutable, so changes to data inside a function do ordinarily not alter the state of data outside that function. But R does allow side effects, such as printing data or making plots, and, of course, allows variables to change values.

Pure functions have no side effects, so a function called with the same input will always return the same output. Pure functions are easier to debug and to reason about because of this. They can be reasoned about in isolation and will not depend on the context in which they are called. The R language does not guarantee that the functions you write are pure, but you can write most of your programs using only pure functions. By keeping your code mostly purely functional, you will write more robust code and code that is easier to modify when the need arises.

You will want to move the impure functions to a small subset of your program. These functions are typically those that need to sample random data or that produce output (either text or plots). If you know where your impure functions are, you know when to be extra careful with modifying code.

The next chapter contains a short introduction to functions in R. Some parts you might already know, and so feel free to skip ahead, but I give a detailed description of how functions are defined and used to ensure that we are all on the same page. The following chapters then move on to more complex issues.

CHAPTER 2

Functions in R

In this chapter, we cover how to write functions in R. If you already know much of what is covered, feel free to skip ahead. We will discuss the way parameters are passed to functions as "promises," a way of passing parameters known as lazy evaluation. If you are not familiar with that but know how to write functions, you can jump forward to that section. We will also cover how to write infix operators and replacement functions, so if you do not know what those are, and how to write them, you can skip ahead to those sections. If you are new to R functions, continue reading from here.

Writing Functions in R

You create an R function using the `function` keyword or, since R 4.1, the `\()` syntax. For example, we can write a function that squares numbers like this:

```
square <- function(x) x**2
```

or like this:

```
square <- \(x) x**2
```

and then use it like this:

```
square(1:5)
## [1]  1  4  9 16 25
```

© Thomas Mailund 2023
T. Mailund, *Functional Programming in R 4*, https://doi.org/10.1007/978-1-4842-9487-1_2

The shorter syntax, \(x) x**2, is intended for so-called "lambda expressions," and the backslash notation is supposed to look like the Greek letter lambda, λ. Lambda expressions are useful when we need to provide short functions as arguments to other functions, which is something we return to in later chapters. Usually, we use the `function()` syntax when defining reusable functions, and I will stick to this notation in every case where we define and name a function the way we did for `square` earlier.

The function we have written takes one argument, x, and returns the result x**2. The return value of a function is always the last expression evaluated in it. If you write a function with a single expression, you can write it as earlier, but for more complex functions, you will typically need several statements in it. If you do, you can put the function's body in curly brackets like this:

```
square <- function(x) {
    x**2
}
```

The following function needs the curly brackets since it needs three separate statements to compute its return value, one for computing the mean of its input, one for getting the standard deviation, and a final expression that returns the input scaled to be centered on the mean and having one standard deviation.

```
rescale <- function(x) {
    m <- mean(x)
    s <- sd(x)
    (x - m) / s
}
```

The first two statements are just there to define some variables we can use in the final expression. This is typical for writing short functions.

Variables you assign to inside a function will only be visible from inside the function. When the function completes its execution, the variables cease to exist. From inside a function, you can see the so-called *local* variables—the function arguments and the variables you assign to in the function body—and you can see the so-called *global* variables—those assigned to outside of the function. Outside of the function, however, you can only see the global variables. At least that is a good way to think about which variables you can see at any point in a program until we get to the gritty details in Chapter 4. For now, think in terms of global variables and local variables, where anything you write outside a function is in the first category and can be seen by anyone, and where function parameters and variables assigned to inside functions are in the second category; see Figure 2-1. If you have the same name for both a global and a local variable, as in the figure where we have a global variable x and a function parameter x, then the name always refers to the local variable.

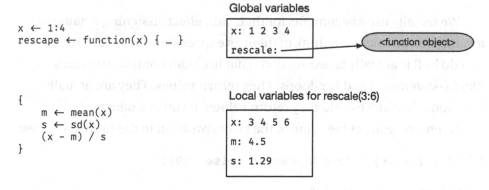

Figure 2-1. *Local and global variables*

Assignments are really also expressions. They return an object, the value that is being assigned; they just do so quietly. R considers some expressions "invisible," and while they do evaluate to some value or other—all expressions do—R does not print the result. Assignments are invisible in this way; they do return to the value on the right-hand side of the assignment, but R makes the result invisible. You can remove this invisibility by putting an assignment in parentheses. The parentheses make R remove the invisibility of the expression result, so you see the actual value:

```
(x <- 1:5)
```

```
## [1]  1  2  3  4  5
```

You can also go the other way and make a value invisible. When you evaluate an expression, R will print it:

```
x**2
```

```
## [1]  1  4  9  16  25
```

but if you put the expression in a call to `invisible`, R will not print the result:

```
invisible(x**2)
```

We usually use assignments for their side effect, assigning a name to a value, so you might not think of them as expressions, but everything you do in R is actually an expression. That includes control structures like if-statements and for-loops. They return values. They are actually functions themselves, and they return values. If you evaluate an if-statement, you get the value of the last expression in the branch it takes:

```
if (2 + 2 == 4) "Brave New World" else "1984"
```

```
## [1] "Brave New World"
```

If you evaluate a loop, you get the value NULL (and not the last expression in its body):

```
x <- for (i in 1:10) i
x
```

```
## NULL
```

Even parentheses and subscripting are functions. Parentheses evaluate to the value you put inside them (but stripped of invisibility), and subscripting, [...] or [[...]], evaluates to some appropriate value on the data structure you are accessing (and you can define how this will work for your own data structures if you want to).

If you want to return a value from a function before its last expression, you can use the return function. It might look like a keyword, but it *is* a function, and you need to include the parentheses when you use it. Many languages will let you return a value by writing

```
return expression
```

Not R. In R, you need to write

```
return(expression)
```

If you are trying to return a value, this will not cause you much trouble. R will tell you that you have a syntax error if you use the former and not the latter syntax. Where it can be a problem is if you want to return from a function without providing a value (in which case the function automatically returns NULL).

If you write something like this:

```
f <- function(x) {
  if (x < 0) return;
  # Something else happens here...
}
```

you will not return if x is negative. The if-expression evaluates to the function return, which is not what you want. Instead, you must write

```
f <- function(x) {
  if (x < 0) return();
  # Something else happens here...
}
```

CHAPTER 2   FUNCTIONS IN R

If x is negative, we call `return()`, which will return NULL. (To return a value, `val`, use `return(val)`).

Return is usually used to exit a function early and isn't used that much in most R code. It is easier to return a value by just making it the last expression in a function than it is to explicitly use `return`. But you can use it to return early like this:

```
rescale <- function(x, only_translate) {
    m <- mean(x)
    translated <- x - m
    if (only_translate) return(translated)
    s <- sd(x)
    translated / s
}
rescale(1:4, TRUE)

## [1] -1.5 -0.5  0.5  1.5

rescale(1:4, FALSE)

## [1] -1.1618950 -0.3872983  0.3872983  1.1618950
```

This function has two arguments, x and only_translate. Your functions can have any number of parameters. When a function takes many arguments, however, it becomes harder to remember in which order you have to put them. To get around that problem, R allows you to provide the arguments to a function using their names. So the two function calls earlier can also be written as

```
rescale(x = 1:4, only_translate = TRUE)
rescale(x = 1:4, only_translate = FALSE)
```

Named Parameters and Default Parameters

If you use named arguments, the order doesn't matter, so this is also equivalent to these function calls:

```
rescale(only_translate = TRUE, x = 1:4)
rescale(only_translate = FALSE, x = 1:4)
```

You can mix positional and named arguments. The positional arguments have to come in the same order as used in the function definition, and the named arguments can come in any order. All the following four function calls are equivalent:

```
rescale(1:4, only_translate = TRUE)
rescale(only_translate = TRUE, 1:4)
rescale(x = 1:4, TRUE)
rescale(TRUE, x = 1:4)
```

When you provide a named argument to a function, you don't need to use the full parameter name. Any unique prefix will do. So we could also have used the following two function calls:

```
rescale(1:4, o = TRUE)
rescale(o = TRUE, 1:4)
```

This is convenient for interactive work with R because it saves some typing, but I do not recommend it when you are writing programs. It can easily get confusing, and if the author of the function adds a new argument to the function with the same prefix as the one you use, it will break your code. If the function author provides a default value for that parameter, your code will *not* break if you use the full argument name. Not breaking, in a situation like this, is a whole lot worse than breaking, because the code will not do the right thing and you will not be immediately aware of that.

Now, default parameters are provided when the function is defined. We could have given `rescale` a default parameter for `only_translate` like this:

```
rescale <- function(x, only_translate = FALSE) {
    m <- mean(x)
    translated <- x - m
    if (only_translate) return(translated)
    s <- sd(x)
    translated / s
}
```

Then, if we call the function, we only need to provide x if we are happy with the default value for `only_translate`.

```
rescale(1:4)
```

```
## [1] -1.1618950 -0.3872983  0.3872983  1.1618950
```

R makes heavy use of default parameters. Many commonly used functions, such as plotting functions and model fitting functions, have lots of arguments. These arguments let you control in great detail what the functions do, making them very flexible, and because they have default values, you usually only have to worry about a few of them.

The "Gobble Up Everything Else" Parameter: "..."

There is a special parameter all functions can take called . . . . This parameter is typically used to pass parameters on to functions *called within* a function. To give an example, we can use it to deal with missing values, NA, in the `rescale` function.

We can write (where I'm building from the shorter version)

```r
rescale <- function(x, ...) {
    m <- mean(x, ...)
    s <- sd(x, ...)
    (x - m) / s
}
```

If we give this function a vector x that contains missing values, it will return NA:

```r
x <- c(NA, 1:3)
rescale(x)
```

```
## [1] NA NA NA NA
```

It would also have done that before because that is how the functions mean and sd work. But both of these functions take an additional parameter, na.rm, that will make them remove all NA values before they do their computations. Our rescale function can do the same now:

```r
rescale(x, na.rm = TRUE)
```

```
## [1]   NA -1  0  1
```

The first value in the output is still NA. Rescaling an NA value can't be anything else. But the rest are rescaled values where that NA was ignored when computing the mean and standard deviation.

The "..." parameter allows a function to take any named parameter at all. If you write a function without it, it will only take the predetermined parameters, but if you add this parameter, it will accept any named parameter at all:

```r
f <- function(x) x
g <- function(x, ...) x
f(1:4, foo = "bar")
```

```
## Error in f(1:4, foo = "bar"): unused argument (foo = "bar")

g(1:4, foo = "bar")

## [1] 1 2 3 4
```

If you then call another function with "..." as a parameter, then all the parameters the first function doesn't know about will be passed on to the second function:

```
f <- function(...) list(...)
g <- function(x, y, ...) f(...)
g(x = 1, y = 2, z = 3, w = 4)

## $z
## [1] 3
##
## $w
## [1] 4
```

In the preceding example, function f creates a list of named elements from "...", and as you can see, it gets the parameters that g doesn't explicitly take.

Using "..." is not particularly safe. It is often very hard to figure out what it actually does in a particular piece of code. What is passed on to other functions depends on what the first function explicitly takes as arguments, and when you call a second function using it, you pass along all the parameters in it. If the function you call doesn't know how to deal with them, you get an error:

```
f <- function(w) w
g <- function(x, y, ...) f(...)
g(x = 1, y = 2, z = 3, w = 4)

## Error in f(...): unused argument (z = 3)
```

In the `rescale` function, it would have been much better to add the `rm.na` parameter explicitly.

That being said, "`...`" is frequently used in R. Particularly because many functions take very many parameters with default values, and adding these parameters to all functions calling them would be tedious and error-prone. It is also the best way to add parameters when specializing generic functions, which is a topic for another book, *Advanced Object-Oriented Programming in R*, by yours truly.

Lazy Evaluation

Expressions used in a function call are not evaluated before they are passed to the function. Most common languages have so-called pass-by-value semantics, which means that all expressions given to parameters of a function are evaluated before the function is called. In R, the semantic is "call-by-promise," also known as "lazy evaluation."

When you call a function and give it expressions as its arguments, these are not evaluated at that point. What the function gets is not the result of evaluating them but the actual expressions, called "promises" (they are promises of an evaluation to a value you can get when you need it), thus the term "call-by-promise." These expressions are only evaluated when they are actually needed, thus the term "lazy evaluation."

This has several consequences for how functions work. First of all, an expression that isn't used in a function isn't evaluated:

```
f <- function(a, b) a
f(2, stop("error if evaluated"))
```

```
## [1] 2
```

```
f(stop("error if evaluated"), 2)
```

```
## Error in f(stop("error if evaluated"), 2): error if
evaluated
```

If you have a parameter that can only be meaningfully evaluated in certain contexts, it is safe enough to have it as a parameter as long as you only refer to it when those necessary conditions are met.

It is also very useful for default values of parameters. These are evaluated inside the scope of the function, so you can write default values that depend on other parameters:

```r
f <- function(a, b = a) a + b
f(a = 2)
```

```
## [1] 4
```

This does *not* mean that all the expressions are evaluated inside the scope of the function, though. We discuss scopes in Chapter 4, but for now, you can think of two scopes: the global scope where global variables live and the function scope that has parameters and local variables as well.

If you call a function like this:

```r
f(a = 2, b = a)
```

you will get an error if you expect b to be the same as a inside the function. If you are lucky and there isn't any global variable called a, you will get a runtime error. If you are unlucky and there *is* a global variable called a, that is what b will be assigned, and if you expect it to be set to 2 here, your code will just give you an incorrect answer.

However, it is safe for a default parameter to be an expression that uses some of the other function arguments. The default parameters are evaluated after the function is called, where they have access to the other arguments. An expression you use when calling a function, however, doesn't see the local variables inside the function, but the variables you have in the calling scope.

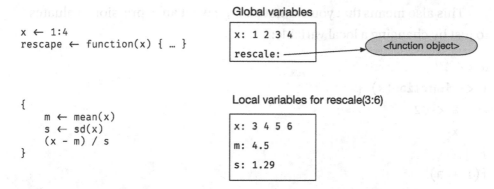

```
x ← 1:4
rescape ← function(x) { … }
```

Global variables

```
x: 1 2 3 4
rescale: ────────────────→  <function object>
```

```
{
    m ← mean(x)
    s ← sd(x)
    (x - m) / s
}
```

Local variables for rescale(3:6)

```
x: 3 4 5 6
m: 4.5
s: 1.29
```

Figure 2-2. *Where arguments and default arguments are evaluated*

Consider Figure 2-2. We have a function, f, that takes two arguments, a and b, where b has a default of 2*a. If we call it as f(2*a, b = 2*a), then both arguments will be expressions that R knows have to be evaluated in the global scope where a is the list 1 2 3 4 5 and where we don't have a b. Neither parameter will be evaluated until we look at the arguments, but when we do, both will be evaluated and to the same value since both are 2*a and a refers to the global a. If, however, we call f as f(2*a) so b gets the default value, we are in a different situation. Inside the function call, a still refers to the expression 2*a to be evaluated in the global scope, but b, also still referring to the expression 2*a, will be evaluated in the *local* scope. So, if we evaluate b, we will first evaluate the parameter a to get 2*a (evaluated using the global a) 2 4 6 8 10, and then we evaluate 2*a with this local a to get 4 8 12 16 20.

So, while arguments aren't evaluated yet when you call a function, they will be when you access them. If they are default arguments, you evaluate them inside the function, and if they were provided in the function call, you evaluated them outside the call, where the function was called.

This also means that you cannot change what an expression evaluates to just by changing a local variable:

```
a <- 4
f <- function(x) {
    a <- 2
    x
}
f(1 + a)

## [1] 5
```

In this example, the expression 1 + a is evaluated inside f, but the a in the expression is the a outside of f and not the a local variable inside f.

This is of course what you want. If expressions really *were* evaluated inside the scope of the function, then you would have no idea what they evaluated to if you called a function with an expression. It would depend on any local variables the function might use.

Because expressions are evaluated in the calling scope and not the scope of the function, you mostly won't notice the difference between call-by-value and call-by-promise. There are certain cases where the difference can bite you, though, if you are not careful.

As an example, we can consider this function:

```
f <- function(a) function(b) a + b
```

This might look a bit odd if you are not used to it, but it is a function that returns another function. We will see many examples of this kind of functions in later chapters.

When we call f with a parameter a, we get a function back that will add a to its argument:

```
f(2)(2)

## [1] 4
```

We can create a list of functions from this f:

```r
ff <- vector("list", 4)
for (i in 1:4) {
  ff[[i]] <- f(i)
}
ff

## [[1]]
## function(b) a + b
## <bytecode: 0x7fe446ad68a8>
## <environment: 0x7fe446a07ca0>
##
## [[2]]
## function(b) a + b
## <bytecode: 0x7fe446ad68a8>
## <environment: 0x7fe446ad71e8>
##
## [[3]]
## function(b) a + b
## <bytecode: 0x7fe446ad68a8>
## <environment: 0x7fe446ad7098>
##
## [[4]]
## function(b) a + b
## <bytecode: 0x7fe446ad68a8>
## <environment: 0x7fe446ad6f48>
```

Here, ff contains four functions, and the idea is that the first of these adds 1 to its argument, the second adds 2, and so on.

If we call the functions in ff, however, weird stuff happens:

```
ff[[1]](1)
```

```
## [1] 5
```

When we get the element ff[[1]], we get the first function we created in the loop. If we substitute into f the value we gave in the call, this is

```
function(b) i + b
```

The parameter a from f has been set to the parameter we gave it, i, but i has not been evaluated at this point!

When we call the function, the expression is evaluated, in the global scope, but there i now has the value 4 because that is the last value it was assigned in the loop. The value of i was 1 when we called it to create the function, but it is 5 when the expression is actually evaluated.

This also means that we can change the value of i before we evaluate one of the functions, and this changes it from the value we intended when we created the function:

```
i <- 1
ff[[2]](1)
```

```
## [1] 2
```

This laziness is only in effect the first time we call the function. If we change i again and call the function, we get the same value as the first time the function was evaluated:

```
i <- 2
ff[[2]](1)
```

```
## [1] 2
```

We can see this in effect by looping over the functions and evaluating them:

```
results <- vector("numeric", 4)
for (i in 1:4) {
  results[i] <- ff[[i]](1)
}
results
```

```
## [1] 5 2 4 5
```

We have already evaluated the first two functions, so they are stuck at the values they got at the time of the first evaluation. The other two get the intended functionality but only because we are setting the variable i in the loop where we evaluate the functions. If we had used a different loop variable, we wouldn't have been so lucky.

This problem is caused by having a function with an unevaluated expression that depends on variables in the outer scope. Functions that return functions are not uncommon, though, if you want to exploit the benefits of having a functional language. It is also a consequence of allowing variables to change values, something most functional programming languages do not allow for such reasons. You cannot entirely avoid it, though, by avoiding for-loops. If you call functions that loop for you, you do not necessarily have control over how they do that, and you can end up in the same situation.

The way to avoid the problem is to force an evaluation of the parameter. If you evaluate it once, it will remember the value, and the problem is gone.

You can do that by just writing the parameter as a single statement. That will evaluate it. It is better to use the function force though, to make it explicit that this is what you are doing. It really just gives you the expression back, so it works exactly as if you just wrote the parameter, but the code makes clear why you are doing it.

If you do this, the problem is gone:

```r
f <- function(a) {
  force(a)
  function(b) a + b
}

ff <- vector("list", 4)
for (i in 1:4) {
  ff[[i]] <- f(i)
}
ff[[1]](1)

## [1] 2

i <- 1
ff[[2]](1)

## [1] 3
```

Functions Don't Have Names

The last thing I want to stress when we talk about defining functions is that functions do not have names. Variables have names, and variables can refer to functions, but these are two separate things.

In many languages, such as Java, Python, or C++, you define a function, and at the same time, you give it an argument. When possible at all, you need a special syntax to define a function without a name.

Not so in R. In R, functions do not have names, and when you define them, you are not giving them a name. We have given names to all the functions we have used earlier by assigning them to variables right where we defined them. We didn't have to. It is the "function(...) ..." syntax that defines a function. We are defining a function whether we assign it to a variable or not.

We can define a function and call it immediately like this:

```
(function(x) x**2)(2)
```

```
## [1] 4
```

We would never do this, of course. Anywhere we would want to define an anonymous function and immediately call it, we could instead just put the body of the function. Functions we want to reuse we *have* to give a name so we can get to them again.

The syntax for defining functions, however, doesn't force us to give them names. When you start to write higher-order functions, that is, functions that take other functions as input or return functions, this is convenient.

Such higher-order functions are an important part of functional programming, and we will see much of them later in the book.

Vectorized Functions

Expressions in R are vectorized. When you write an expression, it is implicitly working on vectors of values, not single values. Even simple expressions that only involve numbers really are vector operations. They are just vectors of length 1.

For longer vectors, expressions work component-wise. So if you have vectors x and y, you can subtract the first from the second component-wise just by writing x - y:

```
x <- 1:5
y <- 6:10
x - y
```

```
## [1] -5 -5 -5 -5 -5
```

If the vectors are not of the same length, the shorter vector is just repeated as many times as is necessary. This is why you can, for example, multiply a number to a vector:

```
2 * x
```

```
## [1]  2  4  6  8 10
```

Here, 2 is a vector of length 1 and x a vector of length 5, and 2 is just repeated five times. You will get a warning if the length of the longer vector is not divisible by the length of the shorter vector, and you generally want to avoid this. The semantic is the same, though: R just keeps repeating the shorter vector as many times as needed.

```
x <- 1:6
y <- 1:3
x - y
```

```
## [1] 0 0 0 3 3 3
```

Depending on how a function is written, it can also be used in vectorized expressions. R is happy to use the result of a function call in a vector expression as long as this result is a vector. This is not quite the same as the function operating component-wise on vectors. Such functions we can call *vectorized* functions.

Most mathematical functions such as sqrt, log, cos, and sin are vectorized, and you can use them in expressions:

```
log(1:3) - sqrt(1:3)
```

```
## [1] -1.0000000 -0.7210664 -0.6334385
```

Functions you write yourself will also be vectorized if their body consists only of vectorized expressions:

```
f <- function(a, b) log(a) - sqrt(b)
f(1:3, 1:3)
```

```
## [1] -1.0000000 -0.7210664 -0.6334385
```

The very first function we wrote in this book, square, was also a vectorized function. The function scale was also, although the functions it used, mean and sd, are not; they take vector input but return a summary of the entire vector and do not operate on the vector component-wise.

A function that uses control structures usually will not be vectorized. We can write a comparison function that returns -1 if the first argument is smaller than the second and 1 if the second is larger than the first, and zero otherwise like this:

```
compare <- function(x, y) {
    if (x < y) {
        -1
    } else if (y < x) {
        1
    } else {
        0
    }
}
```

This function will work fine on single values but not on vectors. The problem is that the if-expression only looks at the first element in the logical vector x < y. (Yes, x < y is a vector because < is a vectorized function.)

To handle if-expressions, we can get around this problem by using the ifelse function. This is a vectorized function that behaves just as an if-else-expression:

```
compare <- function(x, y) {
    ifelse(x < y, -1, ifelse(y < x, 1, 0))
}
compare(1:6, 1:3)
```

```
## [1] 0 0 0 1 1 1
```

The situation is not always so simple that we can replace if-statements with ifelse. In most cases, we can, but when we cannot, we can instead use the function Vectorize. This function takes a function that can operate on single values and translate it into a function that can work component-wise on vectors.

As an example, we can take the compare function from before and vectorize it:

```
compare <- function(x, y) {
    if (x < y) {
        -1
    } else if (y < x) {
        1
    } else {
        0
    }
}
compare <- Vectorize(compare)
compare(1:6, 1:3)
```

```
## [1] 0 0 0 1 1 1
```

By default, Vectorize will vectorize on all parameters of a function. As an example, imagine that we want a scale function that doesn't scale all variables in a vector by the same vector's mean and standard deviation but use the mean and standard deviation of another vector:

```
Scale_with <- function(x, y) {
    (x - mean(y)) / sd(y)
}
```

This function is already vectorized on its first parameter since it just consists of a vectorized expression, but if we use Vectorize on it, we break it:

```
scale_with(1:6, 1:3)

## [1] -1  0  1  2  3  4

scale_with <- Vectorize(scale_with)
scale_with(1:6, 1:3)

## [1] NA NA NA NA NA NA
```

The function we create with Vectorize is vectorized for both x and y, which means that it operates on these component-wise. When scaling, the function only sees one component of y, not the whole vector. The result is a vector of missing values, NA because the standard deviation of a single value is not defined.

We can fix this by explicitly telling Vectorize which parameters should be vectorized—in this example, only parameter x:

```
Scale_with <- function(x, y) {
    (x - mean(y)) / sd(y)
}
scale_with <- Vectorize(scale_with, vectorize.args="x")
scale_with(1:6, 1:3)

## [1] -1  0  1  2  3  4
```

Simple functions are usually already vectorized, or can easily be made vectorized using `ifelse`, but for functions more complex, the `Vectorize` function is needed.

As an example, we can consider a tree data structure and a function for computing the node depth of a named node—the node depth defined as the distance from the root. For simplicity, we consider only binary trees. We can implement trees using lists:

```
Make_node <- function(name, left = NULL, right = NULL)
  list(name = name, left = left, right = right)

tree <- make_node("root",
                  make_node("C", make_node("A"),
                                 make_node("B")),
                  make_node("D"))
```

To compute the node depth, we can traverse the tree recursively:

```
node_depth <- function(tree, name, depth = 0) {
    if (is.null(tree)) return(NA)
    if (tree$name == name) return(depth)

    left <- node_depth(tree$left, name, depth + 1)
    if (!is.na(left)) return(left)
    right <- node_depth(tree$right, name, depth + 1)
    return(right)
}
```

This is not an unreasonably complex function, but it is a function that is harder to vectorize than the `scale_with` function. As it is, it works well for single names:

```
node_depth(tree, "D")
```

```
## [1] 1
```

```
node_depth(tree, "A")
```

```
## [1] 2
```

but you will get an error if you call it on a sequence of names:

```
node_depth(tree, c("A", "B", "C", "D"))
```

It is not hard to imagine that a vectorized version could be useful, however. For example, to get the depth of a sequence of names:

```
node_depth <- Vectorize(node_depth, vectorize.args = "name",
                        USE.NAMES = FALSE)
node_depth(tree, c("A", "B", "C", "D"))
```

```
## [1] 2 2 1 1
```

Here, the USE.NAMES = FALSE is needed to get a simple vector out. If we did not include it, the vector would have names based on the input variables. See the documentation for Vectorize for details.

Infix Operators

Infix operators in R are also functions. You can overwrite them with other functions (but you really shouldn't since you could mess up a lot of code), and you can also make your own infix operators.

User-defined infix operators are functions with special names. A function with a name that starts and ends with % will be considered an infix operator by R. There is no special syntax for creating a function to be used as an infix operator, except that it should take two arguments. There is a special syntax for assigning variables, though, including variables with names starting and ending with %.

27

To work with special variables, you need to quote them with backticks. You cannot write +(2, 2) even though + is a function. R will not understand this as a function call when it sees it written like this. But you can take + and quote it, `+`, and then it is just a variable name like all other variable names:

```
`+`(2, 2)
## [1] 4
```

The same goes for all other infix operators in R and even control structures:

```
`if`(2 > 3, "true", "false")
## [1] "false"
```

The R parser recognizes control structure keywords and various operators, for example, the arithmetic operators, and therefore these get to have a special syntax. But they are all really just functions. Even parentheses are a special syntax for the function `(`, and the subscript operators are as well, `[` and `[[`, respectively. If you quote them, you get a variable name that you can use just like any other function name.

Just like all these operators have a special syntax, variables starting and ending with % get a special syntax. R expects them to be infix operators and will treat an expression like this:

```
exp1 %op% exp2
```

as the function call

```
`%op%`(exp1, exp2)
```

Knowing that you can translate an operator name into a function name just by quoting it also tells you how to define new infix operators. If you assign a function to a variable name, you can refer to it by that name.

If that name is a quoted special name, it gets to use the special syntax for that name.

So, to define an operator %x% that does multiplication, we can write

```
`%x%` <- `*`
3 %x% 2
```

```
## [1] 6
```

Here, we used quotes twice, first to get a variable name we could assign to for %x% and once to get the function that the multiplication operator, *, points to.

Just because all control structures and operators in R are functions that you can overwrite, you shouldn't go doing that without extreme caution. You should *never* change the functions the control structures point to, and you should not change the other operators unless you are defining operators on new types where it is relatively safe to do so. Defining entirely new infix operators, however, can be quite useful if they simplify expressions you write often.

As an example, let us do something else with the %x% operator—after all, there is no point in having two different operators for multiplication. We can make it replicate the left-hand side a number of times given by the right-hand side:

```
`%x%` <- function(expr, num) replicate(num, expr)
3 %x% 5
```

```
## [1] 3 3 3 3 3
```

```
cat("This is ", "very " %x% 3, "much fun")
```

```
## This is  very  very  very  much fun
```

We are using the `replicate` function to achieve this. It does the same thing. It repeatedly evaluates an expression a fixed number of times. Using %x% infix might give more readable code, depending on your taste.

In the interest of honesty, I must mention, though, that we haven't just given `replicate` a new name here, switching of arguments aside. The `%x%` operator works slightly differently. In `%x%`, the `expr` parameter is evaluated when we call `replicate`. So if we call `%x%` with a function that samples random numbers, we will get the same result repeated `num` times; we will not sample `num` times.

```
rnorm(1) %x% 4
```

```
## [1] -0.8094755 -0.8094755 -0.8094755 -0.8094755
```

Lazy evaluation only takes you so far.

To actually get the same behavior as `replicate`, we need a little more trickery:

```
`%x%` <- function(expr, num) {
  m <- match.call()
  replicate(num, eval.parent(m$expr))
}
rnorm(1) %x% 4
```

```
## [1]  0.8430961 -2.9336330 -1.1009706  0.2947148
```

Here, the `match.call` function just gets us a representation of the current function call from which we can extract the expression without evaluating it. We then use `replicate` to evaluate it a number of times in the calling function's scope.

If you don't quite get this, don't worry. We cover scopes in a later chapter.

Replacement Functions

Another class of functions with special names is the so-called *replacement functions*. Data in R is immutable. You can change what data parameters point to, but you cannot change the actual data. Even when it looks like you are modifying data, you are, at least conceptually, creating a copy, modifying that, and making a variable point to the new copy.

We can see this in a simple example with vectors. If we create two vectors that point to the same initial vector, and then modify one of them, the other remains unchanged:

```
x <- y <- 1:5
x
```

```
## [1] 1 2 3 4 5
```

```
y
```

```
## [1] 1 2 3 4 5
```

```
x[1] <- 6
x
```

```
## [1] 6 2 3 4 5
```

```
y
```

```
## [1] 1 2 3 4 5
```

R is smart about it. It won't make a copy of values if it doesn't have to. Semantically, it is best to think of any modification as creating a copy, but for performance reasons, R will only make a copy when it is necessary—at least for built-in data like vectors. Typically, this happens when you have two variables referring to the same data, and you "modify" one of them.

We can use the `address` function to get the memory address of an object. This will change when a copy is made but will remain the same when it isn't. And we can use the `mem_change` function from the `pryr` package to see how much memory is allocated for an expression. Using these two functions, we can dig a little deeper into this copying mechanism. (The exact output will depend on your computer, but you should see something similar to what is shown as follows.)

We can start by creating a longish vector and modifying it:

```
library(pryr)

rm(x) ; rm(y)
mem_change(x <- 1:10000000)
```

```
## 2.31 kB
```

```
address(x)
```

```
## [1] "0x7fe426826a90"
```

```
mem_change(x[1] <- 6)
```

```
## 80 MB
```

```
address(x)
```

```
## [1] "0x7fe420000000"
```

When we assign to the first element in this vector, we see that the entire vector is being copied. This might look odd since I just told you that R would only copy a vector if it had to, and here we are just modifying an element in it, and no other variable refers to it.

The reason we get a copy here is that the expression we used to create the vector, `1:10000000`, creates an integer vector. The value 6 we assign to the first element is a floating point, called "numeric" in R. If we want an actual integer, we have to write "L" (for "long" integer) after the number:

```
class(6)
```

```
## [1] "numeric"
```

```
class(6L)
```

```
## [1] "integer"
```

When we assign a numeric to an integer vector, R has to convert the entire vector into numeric, and that is why we get a copy:

```
z <- 1:5
class(z)
```

```
## [1] "integer"
```

```
z[1] <- 6
class(z)
```

```
## [1] "numeric"
```

If we assign another numeric to it, after it has been converted, we no longer get a copy:

```
mem_change(x[3] <- 8)
```

```
## -1.14 kB
```

```
address(x)
```

```
## [1] "0x7fe420000000"
```

All expression evaluations modify the memory a little, up or down, but the change is much smaller than the entire vector, so we can see that the vector isn't being copied, and the address remains the same.

If we assign x to another variable, we do not get a copy. We just have the two names refer to the same value:

```
mem_change(y <- x)
```

```
## 376 B
```

```
address(x)
```

```
## [1] "0x7fe420000000"
```

```
address(y)
```

```
## [1] "0x7fe420000000"
```

If we change x again, though, we need a copy to make the other vector point to the original, unmodified data:

```
mem_change(x[3] <- 8)
```

```
## 80 MB
```

```
address(x)
```

```
## [1] "0x7fe430000000"
```

```
address(y)
```

```
## [1] "0x7fe420000000"
```

But after that copy, we can again assign to x without making additional copies:

```
mem_change(x[4] <- 9)
```

```
## 112 B
```

```
address(x)
```

```
## [1] "0x7fe430000000"
```

When you assign to a variable in R, you are calling the assignment function, `` `<-` ``. When you assign to an element in a vector or list, you are using the `` `[<-` `` function. But there is a whole class of such functions you can use to make the appearance of modifying an object, without actually doing it of course. These are called replacement functions and have names that end in <-. An example is the `` `names<-` `` function. If you have a vector x, you can give its elements names using this syntax:

```
x <- 1:4
x
```

```
## [1] 1 2 3 4
```

```
names(x) <- letters[1:4]
x
```

```
## a b c d
## 1 2 3 4
```

```
names(x)
```

```
## [1] "a" "b" "c" "d"
```

There are two different functions in play here. The last expression, which gives us x's names, is the names function. The function we use to *assign* the names to x is the `` `names<-` `` function.

Any function you define whose name ends with <- becomes a replacement function, and the syntax for it is that it evaluates whatever is on the right-hand side of the assignment operator and assigns the result to the variable that it takes as its argument.

So this syntax

```
names(x) <- letters[1:4]
```

is translated into

```
x <- `names<-`(x, letters[1:4])
```

No values are harmed in the evaluation of this, but the variable is set to the new value.

We can write our own replacement functions using this syntax. There are just two requirements. The function name has to end with <-—so we need to quote the name when we assign to it—and the argument for the value that goes to the right-hand side of the assignment has to be named value. The last requirement is there, so replacement functions can take more than two arguments.

The `attr<-` function is an example of this. Attributes are key-value maps that can be associated with objects. You can get the attributes associated with an object using the attributes function and set all attributes with the `attributes<-` function, but you can assign individual attributes using `attr<-`. It takes three arguments, the object to modify, a which parameter that is the name of the attribute to set, and the value argument that goes to the right-hand side of the assignment. The which argument is passed to the function on the left-hand side together with the object to modify:

```
x <- 1:4
attributes(x)

## NULL

attributes(x) <- list(foo = "bar")
attributes(x)

## $foo
## [1] "bar"

attr(x, "baz") <- "qux"
attributes(x)

## $foo
## [1] "bar"
##
```

```
## $baz
## [1] "qux"
```

We can write a replacement function to make the tree construction we had earlier in the chapter slightly more readable. Earlier, we constructed the tree like this:

```
tree <- make_node("root",
                  make_node("C", make_node("A"),
                                 make_node("B")),
                  make_node("D"))
```

but we can make functions for setting the children of an object like this:

```
`left<-` <- function(node, value) {
    node$left = value
    node
}
`right<-` <- function(node, value) {
    node$right = value
    node
}
```

and then construct the tree like this:

```
A <- make_node("A")
B <- make_node("B")
C <- make_node("C")
D <- make_node("D")
root <- make_node("root")
left(C) <- A
right(C) <- B
left(root) <- C
```

```
right(root) <- D
tree <- root
```

To see the result, we can write a function for printing a tree. To keep the function simple, I assume that either both children are NULL or both are trees. It is simple to extend it to deal with trees that do not satisfy that; it just makes the function a bit longer:

```
print_tree <- function(tree) {
  build_string <- function(node) {
    if (is.null(node$left) && is.null(node$right)) {
        node$name
    } else {
        left <- build_string(node$left)
        right <- build_string(node$right)
        paste0("(", left, ",", right, ")")
    }
  }
  build_string(tree)
}
print_tree(tree)
```

```
## [1] "((A,B),D)"
```

This function shows the tree in what is known as the Newick format and doesn't show the names of inner nodes, but you can see the structure of the tree.

The order in which we build the tree using children is important. When we set the children for root, we refer to the variable C. If we set the children for C *after* we set the children for root, we get the *old* version of C, not the new modified version:

```
A <- make_node("A")
B <- make_node("B")
C <- make_node("C")
D <- make_node("D")
root <- make_node("root")
left(root) <- C
right(root) <- D
left(C) <- A
right(C) <- B
tree <- root
print_tree(tree)

## [1] "(C,D)"
```

Replacement functions only look like they are modifying data. They are not. They only reassign values to variables.

CHAPTER 3

Pure Functional Programming

A "pure" function is a function that behaves like a mathematical function: it maps values from one space to another, the same value always maps to the same result, and there is no such thing as "side effects" in a mathematical function.

The level to which programming languages go to ensure that functions are pure varies, and R does precious little. Because values are immutable, you have some guarantee about which side effects functions can have, but not much. Functions can modify variables outside their scope, for example, modify global variables. They can print or plot and alter the state of the R process this way. They can also sample random numbers and use them for their computations, making the result of a function nondeterministic, for all intents and purposes, so the same value does not always map to the same result.

Pure functions are desirable because they are easier to reason about. If a function does not have any side effects, you can treat it as a black box that just maps between values. If it has side effects, you will also need to know how it modifies other parts of the program, and that means you have to understand, at least at some level, what the body of the function is doing. If all you need to know about a function is how it maps from input parameters to results, you can change its implementation at any point without breaking any code that relies on the function.

© Thomas Mailund 2023

T. Mailund, *Functional Programming in R 4*, https://doi.org/10.1007/978-1-4842-9487-1_3

Nondeterministic functions, functions whose result is not always the same on the same input, are not necessarily hard to reason about. They are just harder to test and debug if their results depend on random numbers.

Since pure functions are easier to reason about, and to test, you will want to write as much of your programs using pure functions. You cannot necessarily write *all* your programs in pure functions. Sometimes, you need randomness to implement Monte Carlo methods, or sometimes you need functions to produce output. But if you write most of your program using pure functions, and know where the impure functions are, you are writing better and more robust programs.

Writing Pure Functions

There is not much work involved in guaranteeing that a function you write is pure. You should avoid sampling random numbers and stay away from modifying variables outside the scope of the function.

It is trivial to avoid sampling random numbers. Don't call any function that does it, either directly or through other functions. If a function only calls deterministic functions and doesn't introduce any randomness itself, then the function will be deterministic.

It is only slightly less trivial to guarantee that you are not modifying something outside of the scope of a function. You need a special function, <<-, to modify variables outside of a function's local scope (we return to this operator in the next chapter), so avoid using that. Then all assignments will be to local variables, and you cannot modify variables in other scopes. If you avoid this operator, then the only risk you have of modifying functions outside of your scope is through lazy evaluation. Remember the example from the previous chapter where we created a list of functions. The functions contained unevaluated expressions whose values depended on a variable we were changing before we evaluated the expressions.

Strictly speaking, we would still have a pure function if we returned functions with such an unevaluated expression that depended on local variables. Even the functions we would be returning would be pure. They would be referring to local variables in the first function, variables that cannot be changed without the <<- operator once the first function returns. They just wouldn't necessarily be the functions you intended to return.

While such a function would be pure by the strict definition, they do have the problem that the functions we return depend on the state of local variables inside the first function. From a programming perspective, it doesn't much help us that the functions are pure if they are hard to reason about, and in this case, we would need to know how changing the state in the first function affects the functionality of the others.

A solution to avoid problems with functions depending on variables outside their own scope, that is, variables that are not either arguments or local variables, is to simply never change what a variable refers to.

Programming languages that guarantee that functions are pure enforce this. There simply isn't any way to modify the value of a variable. You can define constants, but there is no such thing as variables. Since R does have variables, you will have to avoid assigning to the same variable more than once if you want to guarantee that your functions are pure in this way.

It is very easy to accidentally reuse a variable name in a long function, even if you never intended to change the value of a variable. Keeping your functions short and simple alleviates this somewhat, but there is no way to guarantee that it doesn't happen. The only control structure that actually forces you to change variables is for-loops. You simply cannot write a for-loop without having a variable to loop over.

Now for-loops have a bad reputation in R, and many will tell you to avoid them because they are slow. This is not true. They are slow compared to loops in more low-level languages, but this has nothing to do with them being loops. Because R is a very dynamic language where everything you do involves calling functions, and functions that can be changed at any point if someone redefines a variable, R code is just generally slow. When you call built-in functions like sum or mean, they are fast because they are implemented in C. By using vectorized expressions and built-in functions, you do not pay the penalty of the dynamism. If you write a loop yourself in R, then you do. You pay the same price, however, if you use some of the other constructions that people recommend instead of loops; constructions we will return to in Chapter 6.

The real reason you should use such other constructions is that they make the intent behind your code clearer than a loop will do, at least once you get familiar with functional programming, and because you avoid the looping variable that can cause problems. The reason people often find that their loops are inefficient is that it is very easy to write loops that "modify" data, forcing R to make copies. This problem doesn't go away just because we avoid loops and is something we return to later toward the end of this chapter.

Recursion As Loops

The way functional programming languages avoid loops is by using recursion instead. Anything you can write as a loop you can also write using recursive function calls, and most of this chapter will be focusing on getting used to thinking in terms of recursive functions.

Thinking of problems as recursive is not just a programming trick for avoiding loops. It is generally a method of breaking problems into simpler subproblems that are easier to solve. When you have to address a problem, you can first consider whether there are base cases that are trivial to solve. If we want to search for an element in a sequence, it is trivial to determine if it is there if the sequence is empty. Then it obviously isn't there. Now, if the sequence isn't empty, we have a harder problem, but we can break it into two smaller problems. Is the element we are searching for the first element in the sequence? If so, the element is there. If the first element is not equal to the element we are searching for, then it is only in the sequence if it is the remainder of the sequence.

We can write a linear search function based on this breakdown of the problem. We will first check for the base case and return FALSE if we are searching in an empty sequence. Otherwise, we check the first element; if we find it, we return TRUE, and if it wasn't the first element, we call the function recursively on the rest of the sequence:

```
lin_search <- function(element, sequence) {
    if (is_empty(sequence))                     FALSE
    else if (first(sequence) == element) TRUE
    else lin_search(element, rest(sequence))
}

x <- 1:5
lin_search(0, x)

## [1] FALSE

Lin_search(1, x)

## [1] TRUE

lin_search(5, x)

## [1] TRUE

lin_search(6, x)

## [1] FALSE
```

I have hidden away the test for emptiness, the extraction of the first element, and the remainder of the sequence in three functions: is_empty, first, and rest. For a vector, they can be implemented like this:

```
is_empty <- function(x) length(x) == 0
first <- function(x) x[1]
rest <- function(x) x[-1]
```

A vector is empty if it has length zero. The first element is of course just the first element. The rest function is everything except the first element (and indexing with -1 gets us that).

Now this search algorithm works, but you should never write code like the rest function I just wrote. The way we extract the rest of a vector by slicing will make R copy that subvector. The first time we call rest, we get the entire vector minus the first element, the second time we get the entire vector minus the first two, and so on. This adds up to about half the length of the vector squared. So while the search algorithm should be linear time, the way we extract the rest of a vector makes it run in quadratic time.

In practice, this doesn't matter. There is a limit in R on how deep we can go in recursive calls, and we will reach that limit long before performance becomes an issue. We return to these issues at the end of the chapter, but for now we will just, for aesthetic reasons, avoid a quadratic running time algorithm if we can make a linear time algorithm.

Languages that are built for using recursion instead of loops usually represent sequences in a different way—a way where you can get the rest of a sequence in constant time. We can implement a version of such sequences by representing the elements in the sequence by a structure that has a next variable that points to the remainder of the sequence. Let us call that kind of structure a *next list*. This is an example of a *linked list*, but there are different variants of linked lists, and this one just has a reference to the rest of the sequence, so I will call it a *next list*. We can translate a single element into such a sequence using this function:

```
next_list <- function(element, rest = NULL)
    list(element = element, rest = rest)
```

and construct a sequence by nested calls of the function, similarly to how we constructed a tree in the previous chapter:

```
x <- next_list(1, next_list(2, next_list(3, next_list(4))))
```

For this structure, we can define the functions we need for the search algorithm like this:

```
nl_is_empty <- function(nl) is.null(nl)
nl_first <- function(nl) nl$element
nl_rest <- function(nl) nl$rest
```

and the actual search algorithm like this:

```
nl_lin_search <- function(element, sequence) {
    if (nl_is_empty(sequence))              FALSE
    else if (nl_first(sequence) == element) TRUE
    else nl_lin_search(element, nl_rest(sequence))
}
```

This works fine, and in linear time, but constructing lists is a bit cumbersome. We should write a function for translating a vector into a next list. To construct such function, we can again think recursively. If we have a vector of length zero, the base case, then the next list should be NULL. Otherwise, we want to make a next list where the first element is the first element of the vector, and the rest of the list is the next list of the remainder of the vector:

```
vector_to_next_list <- function(x) {
    if (is_empty(x)) NULL
    else next_list(first(x), vector_to_next_list(rest(x)))
}
```

This works, but, of course, we have just moved the performance problem from the search algorithm to the vector_to_next_list function. This function still needs to get the rest of a vector, and it does it by copying. The translation from vectors to next lists takes quadratic time. We need a way to get the rest of a vector without copying.

One solution is to keep track of an index into the vector. If that index is interpreted as the index where the vector really starts, we can get the rest of the vector just by increasing the index. We could use these helper functions:

```
i_is_empty <- function(x, i) i > length(x)
i_first <- function(x, i) x[i]
```

and write the conversion like this:

```
i_vector_to_next_list <- function(x, i = 1) {
    if (i_is_empty(x, i)) NULL
    else next_list(i_first(x, i), i_vector_to_next_
    list(x, i + 1))
}
```

Of course, with the same trick, we could just have implemented the search algorithm using an index:

```
i_lin_search <- function(element, sequence, i = 1) {
    if (i_is_empty(sequence, i))              FALSE
    else if (i_first(sequence, i) == element) TRUE
    else i_lin_search(element, sequence, i + 1)
}
```

Using the index implementation, we can't really write a rest function. Writing a function that returns a pair of a vector and an index is harder to work with than just incrementing the index itself.

When you write recursive functions on a sequence, the key abstractions you need will be checking if the sequence is empty, getting the first element, and getting the rest of the sequence. Using functions for these three operations doesn't help us unless these functions would let us work on different data types for sequences. It is possible to make such abstractions, but we will not consider it more in this book. Here, we will just implement the abstractions directly in our recursive functions from now on. If we do this, the linear search algorithm simply becomes

```
lin_search <- function(element, sequence, i = 1) {
    if (i > length(sequence)) FALSE
    else if (sequence[i] == element) TRUE
    else lin_search(element, sequence, i + 1)
}
```

The Structure of a Recursive Function

Recursive functions all follow the same pattern: figure out the base cases that are easy to solve and understand how you can break down the problem into smaller pieces that you can solve recursively. It is the same approach that is called "divide and conquer" in algorithm design theory. Reducing a problem to smaller problems is the hard part. There are two things to be careful about: Are the smaller problems *really* smaller? How do you combine solutions from the smaller problems to solve the larger problem?

In the linear search we have worked on so far, we know that the recursive call is looking at a smaller problem because each call is looking at a shorter sequence. It doesn't matter if we implement the function using lists or use an index into a vector, we know that when we call recursively, we are looking at a shorter sequence. For functions working on sequences, this is generally the case, and if you know that each time you call recursively you are moving closer to a base case, you know that the function will eventually finish its computation.

The recursion doesn't always have to be on everything except the first element in a sequence. For a binary search, for example, we can search in logarithmic time in a sorted sequence by reducing the problem to half the size in each recursive call. The algorithm works like this: if you have an empty sequence, you can't find the element you are searching for, so you return FALSE. If the sequence is not empty, you check if the middle element is the element you are searching for, in which case you return TRUE. If it isn't, check if it is smaller than the element you are looking for, in which case you call recursively on the last half of the sequence, and if not, you call recursively on the first half of the sequence.

This sounds simple enough, but first attempts at implementing this often end up calling recursively on the same sequence again and again, never getting closer to finishing. This happens if we are not careful when we pick the first or last half.

This implementation will not work. If you search for 0 or 5, you will get an infinite recursion:

```r
binary_search <- function(element, x,
                          first = 1, last = length(x)) {
    if (last < first) return(FALSE) # empty sequence

    middle <- (last - first) %/% 2 + first
    if (element == x[middle]) {
        TRUE
    } else if (element < x[middle]) {
        binary_search(element, x, first, middle)
    } else {
        binary_search(element, x, middle, last)
    }
}
```

This is because you get a `middle` index that equals `first`, so you call recursively on the same problem you were trying to solve, not a simpler one.

You can solve it by never including `middle` in the range you try to solve recursively—after all, you only call the recursion if you know that `middle` is not the element you are searching for:

```
binary_search <- function(element, x,
                          first = 1, last = length(x)) {

    if (last < first) return(FALSE) # empty sequence

    middle <- (last - first) %/% 2 + first
    if (element == x[middle]) {
        TRUE
    } else if (element < x[middle]) {
        binary_search(element, x, first, middle - 1)
    } else {
        binary_search(element, x, middle + 1, last)
    }
}
```

It is crucial that you make sure that all recursive calls actually are working on a smaller problem. For sequences, that typically means making sure that you call recursively on shorter sequences.

For trees, a data structure that is fundamentally recursive—a tree is either a leaf or an inner node containing a number of children that are themselves also trees—we call recursively on subtrees, thus making sure that we are looking at smaller problems in each recursive call.

The node_depth function we wrote in the first chapter is an example of this:

```
node_depth <- function(tree, name, depth = 0) {
    if (is.null(tree))      return(NA)
    if (tree$name == name) return(depth)

    left <- node_depth(tree$left, name, depth + 1)
    if (!is.na(left)) return(left)
    right <- node_depth(tree$right, name, depth + 1)
    return(right)
}
```

The base cases deal with an empty tree—an empty tree doesn't contain the node we are looking for, so we trivially return NA. If the tree isn't empty, we either have found the node we are looking for, in which case we can return the result. If not, we call recursively on the left tree. We return the result if we found the node we were looking for. Otherwise, we return the result of a recursive call on the right tree (whether we found it or not, if the node wasn't in the tree at all, the final result will be NA).

The functions we have written so far do not combine the results of the subproblems we solve recursively. The functions are all search functions, and the result they return is either directly found or the result one of the recursive functions return. It is not always that simple, and often you need to do something with the result from the recursive call(s) to solve the larger problem.

A simple example is computing the factorial. The factorial of a number n, $n!$, is equal to $n \times (n-1)!$ with a base case $1! = 1$. It is very simple to write a recursive function to return the factorial, but we cannot just return the result of a recursive call. We need to multiply the result we get from the recursive call with n:

```
factorial <- function(n) {
    if (n == 1) 1
    else n * factorial(n - 1)
}
```

Here, I am assuming that n is an integer and n 0. If it is not, the recursion doesn't move us closer to the base case, and we will (in principle) keep going forever. So here is another case where we need to be careful to make sure that when we call recursively, we are actually making progress on solving the problem. In this function, I am only guaranteeing this for positive integers.

In most algorithms, we will need to do something to the results of recursive calls to complete the computation. As another example, besides `factorial`, we can consider a function for removing duplicates in a sequence. Duplicates are elements that are equal to the next element in the sequence. It is similar to the `unique` function built into R except that this function only removes repeated elements that are right next to each other.

To write it, we follow the recipe for writing recursive functions. What is the base case? An empty sequence doesn't have duplicates, so the result is just an empty sequence. The same is the case for a sequence with only one element. Such a sequence does not have duplicated elements, so the result is also the input sequence. If we always know that the input to our function has at least one element, we don't have to worry about the first base case, but if the function might be called on empty sequences, we need to take care of both. For sequences with more than one element, we need to check if the first element equals the next. If it does, we should recurse on the sequence that leaves out the first element, thus removing a duplicated element. If it does not, we should return the first element together with the rest of the sequence where duplicates have been removed.

A solution using "next lists" could look like this:

```
rm_duplicates <- function(x) {
    # Base cases
    if (is.null(x)) return(NULL)
    if (is.null(x$rest)) return(x)

    # Recursive case
    if (x$element == x$rest$element) rm_duplicates(x$rest)
    else next_list(x$element, rm_duplicates(x$rest))
}

x <- next_list(1, next_list(1, next_list(2, next_list(2))))
rm_duplicates(x)

## $element
## [1] 1
##
## $rest
## $rest$element
## [1] 2
##
## $rest$rest
## NULL
```

To get a solution to the general problem, we have to combine the smaller solution we get from the recursive call with information in the larger problem. If the first element is equal to the first element we get back from the recursive call, we have a duplicate and should just return the result of the recursive call; if not, we need to combine the first element with the next list from the recursive call.

We can also implement this function for vectors. To avoid copying vectors each time we remove a duplicate, we can split that function into two parts. First, we find the indices of all duplicates, and then we remove these from the vector in a single operation:

```
vector_rm_duplicates <- function(x) {
    dup <- find_duplicates(x)
    x[-dup]
}
Vector_rm_duplicates(c(1, 1, 2, 2))

## [1] 1 2
```

R already has a built-in function for finding duplicates, called duplicated, and we could implement find_duplicates using it (it returns a boolean vector, but we can use the function which to get the indices of the TRUE values). It is a good exercise to implement it ourselves, though.

```
find_duplicates <- function(x, i = 1) {
    if (i >= length(x)) return(c())

    if (x[i] == x[i + 1]) c(i, find_duplicates(x, i + 1))
    else find_duplicates(x, i + 1)
}
```

The structure is very similar to the list version, but here we return the result of the recursive call together with the current index if it is a duplicate and just the result of the recursive call otherwise.

This solution isn't perfect. Each time we create an index vector by combining it with the recursive result, we are making a copy so the running time will be quadratic in the length of the result. We can turn it into a linear time algorithm in the output as well by making a next list instead of a vector of the indices and then translate that into a vector in the remove duplicates function before we index into the vector x to remove the duplicates. I will leave that as an exercise.

As another example of a recursive function where we need to combine results from recursive calls, we can consider computing the size of a tree. The base case is when it is empty (it is NULL), where the size is zero. The recursive case is the size of the left tree plus the size of the right tree plus one for the node:

55

```r
size_of_tree <- function(node) {
  if (is.null(node)) 0
  else size_of_tree(node$left) + size_of_tree(node$right) + 1
}

make_node <- function(name, left = NULL, right = NULL)
  list(name = name, left = left, right = right)

tree <- make_node("root",
                  make_node("C", make_node("A"),
                                 make_node("B")),
                  make_node("D"))

size_of_tree(tree)

## [1] 5
```

If I wanted to remember the size of subtrees so I didn't have to recompute them, I could attempt something like this:

```r
set_size_of_subtrees <- function(node) {
  if (is.null(node)) return(0); # We can't save
  anything in NULL

  # Compute the size if we don't have it
  if (is.null(node$size)) {
    left_size <- set_size_of_subtrees(node$left)
    right_size <- set_size_of_subtrees(node$right)
    node$size <- left_size + right_size + 1
  }

  return(node$size)
}
```

but remember that data in R cannot be changed. If I run this function on a tree, it would create nodes that knew the size of a subtree, but these nodes would be copies and not the nodes in the tree I call the function on:

```
set_size_of_subtrees(tree)
```

```
## [1] 5
```

```
tree$size
```

```
## NULL
```

To actually remember the sizes, I would have to construct a whole new tree where the nodes knew their size. So I would need this function:

```
# Handles both NULL and nodes that know their size
get_size <- function(node) if (is.null(node)) 0 else node$size

set_size_of_subtrees <- function(node) {
  if (is.null(node)) return(NULL)

  # Update children
  node$left <- set_size_of_subtrees(node$left)
  node$right <- set_size_of_subtrees(node$right)

  # Set size
  node$size <- get_size(node$left) + get_size(node$right) + 1

  return(node)
}
```

```
tree <- set_size_of_subtrees(tree)
tree$size
```

```
## [1] 5
```

Tail-Recursion

Functions, such as our search functions, that return the result of a recursive call without doing further computation on it are called *tail recursive*. Such functions are particularly desired in functional programming languages because they can be translated into loops, removing the overhead involved in calling functions. R, however, unfortunately does not implement this tail-recursion optimization. There are good but technical reasons why, having to do with scopes. This doesn't mean that we cannot exploit tail-recursion and the optimizations possible if we write our functions to be tail-recursive, we just have to translate our functions into loops explicitly. We cover that in the next section. First, I will show you a technique for translating an otherwise not tail-recursive function into one that is.

As long as you have a function that only calls recursively zero or one time, it is a very simple trick. You pass along values in recursive calls that can be used to compute the final value once the recursion gets to a base case.

As a simple example, we can take the factorial function. The way we wrote it earlier was not tail-recursive. We called recursively and then multiplied *n* to the result:

```
factorial <- function(n) {
    if (n == 1) 1
    else n * factorial(n - 1)
}
```

We can translate it into a tail-recursive function by passing the product of the numbers we have seen so far along to the recursive call. Such a value that is passed along is typically called an accumulator. The tail-recursive function would look like this:

```
factorial <- function(n, acc = 1) {
    if (n == 1) acc
    else factorial(n - 1, acc * n)
}
```

Similarly, we can take the find_duplicates function we wrote and turn it into a tail-recursive function. The original function looks like this:

```
find_duplicates <- function(x, i = 1) {
    if (i >= length(x)) return(c())
    rest <- find_duplicates(x, i + 1)
    if (x[i] == x[i + 1]) c(i, rest) else rest
}
```

It needs to return a list of indices so that is what we pass along as the accumulator:

```
find_duplicates <- function(x, i = 1, acc = c()) {
    if (i >= length(x)) return(acc)
    if (x[i] == x[i + 1]) find_duplicates(x, i + 1, c(acc, i))
    else find_duplicates(x, i + 1, acc)
}
```

All functions that call themselves recursively at most once can equally easily be translated into tail-recursive functions using an appropriate accumulator.

It is harder for functions that make more than one recursive call, like the tree functions we wrote earlier. It is not impossible to make them tail-recursive, but it requires a trick called *continuation passing*, which I will show you in Chapter 5.

Runtime Considerations

Now for the bad news. All the techniques I have shown you in this chapter for writing pure functional programs using recursion instead of loops are relatively slow in R.

From a software design perspective, you will want to write pure functions, but relying on recursion instead of loops comes at a runtime cost. We can compare our recursive linear search function with one that uses a for-loop to see how much overhead we incur.

The recursive function looked like this:

```
r_lin_search <- function(element, sequence, i = 1) {
  if (i > length(sequence)) FALSE
  else if (sequence[i] == element) TRUE
  else r_lin_search(element, sequence, i + 1)
}
```

A version using a for-loop could look like this:

```
l_lin_search <- function(element, sequence) {
  for (e in sequence) {
    if (e == element) return(TRUE)
  }
  return(FALSE)
}
```

We can use the function microbenchmark from the microbenchmark package to compare the two. If we search for an element that is not contained in the sequence we search in, we will have to search through the entire sequence, so we can use that worst-case scenario for the performance measure:

```
x <- 1:1000
microbenchmark::microbenchmark(
  r_lin_search(-1, x),
  l_lin_search(-1, x)
)

## Unit: microseconds
##                   expr     min      lq       mean
##   r_lin_search(-1, x ) 834.297 927.9130 1121.50154
##   l_lin_search(-1, x )  20.117  20.6345   47.32387
##   median       uq       max neval cld
##   986.011 1094.573 5361.536   100   b
##    23.087   25.269 2341.506   100   a
```

The recursive function is orders of magnitude slower than the function that uses a loop. Keep that in mind if people tell you that loops are slow in R; they might be, but recursive functions are slower.

It gets worse than that. R has a limit to how deep you can call a function recursively, and if we were searching in a sequence longer than about a thousand elements, we would reach this limit, and R would terminate the call with an error.

This doesn't mean that reading this chapter was a complete waste of time. It can be very useful to think in terms of recursion when you are constructing a function. There is a reason why divide and conquer is frequently used to solve algorithmic problems. You just want to translate the recursive solution into a loop once you have designed the function.

For functions such as linear search, we would never program a solution as a recursive function in the first place. The for-loop version is much easier to write and much more efficient. Other problems are much easier to solve with a recursive algorithm, and there the implementation is also easier done by first thinking in terms of a recursive function. The binary search is an example of such a problem. It is inherently recursive since we solve the search by another search on a shorter string. It is also less likely to hit the allowed recursion limit since it will only call recursively a number of times that is logarithmic in the length of the input, but that is another issue.

The recursive binary search looked like this:

```
r_binary_search <- function(element, x,
                              first = 1, last = length(x)) {
  if (last < first) return(FALSE) # empty sequence

  middle <- (last - first) %/% 2 + first
  if (element == x[middle]) TRUE
  else if (element < x[middle]) {
    r_binary_search(element, x, first, middle - 1)
  } else {
    r_binary_search(element, x, middle + 1, last)
  }
}
```

It is a tail-recursive function, and we can exploit that to translate it into a version that uses a loop instead of recursive calls. To translate a tail-recursive function into a looping function, you put the body of the function in a repeat-loop. A repeat-loop will loop forever unless you explicitly exit from it, but the base case tests in the recursive function can be used to exit the loop using an explicit return call. When you would normally call recursively, you instead just update the local parameters. You simply have to update them to the values they would have if you had called the function recursive. So for the first recursive call earlier, r_binary_search(element, x, first, middle - 1), you have to update element <- element, x <- x, first <- first, and last <- middle - 1, where, of course, there is no need to update the variables that should get their current value, so that update is simply last <- middle - 1. Likewise, for the second recursive call, element, x, and last keep their current value, but first is updated to middle + 1. The result of the rewrite looks like this:

```
l_binary_search <- function(element, x, first = 1, last =
length(x)) {
  repeat {
    # Base case with no match
    if (last < first) return(FALSE) # empty sequence

    middle <- (last - first) %/% 2 + first

    # Base case with a match
    if (element == x[middle]) return(TRUE)

    if (element < x[middle]) {
      last <- middle - 1    # "recursive" call with last =
      middle - 1
    } else {
      first <- middle + 1   # "recursive" call with first =
      middle + 1
    }
  }
}
```

The translation always follows this simple pattern, which is why many programming languages will do it for you automatically.

Once you have rewritten a function like this, using a repeat-loop, you can often simplify it further to get a while loop that you drop out of when you reach a base case, but this is less automatic (although rarely any harder):

```r
l_binary_search <- function(element, x, first = 1, last =
length(x)) {
  while (last >= first) {
    middle <- (last - first) %/% 2 + first

    # Base case with a match
    if (element == x[middle]) return(TRUE)

    if (element < x[middle]) {
      last <- middle - 1    # "recursive" call with last =
      middle - 1
    } else {
      first <- middle + 1   # "recursive" call with first =
      middle + 1
    }
  }
  return(FALSE)
}
```

If your function is *not* tail-recursive, it is a lot more work to translate it into a version that uses loops. You will essentially have to simulate the function call stack yourself. That involves a lot more programming, but it is not functional programming and thus is beyond the scope of this book. Not to worry, though, using continuations, a topic we cover later in the book, you can generally translate your functions into tail-recursive functions and then use a trick called a "trampoline" to replace recursion with loops.

CHAPTER 4

Scope and Closures

A *scope* or *environment* is something functions and expressions are associated with that tells them what value each variable refers to. It is used to figure out which environment expressions are evaluated in. The same variable name can be used in many places in a program, referring to different things in different locations, but the scope of an expression tells R exactly how to map names to values. In R, you have both implicit environments—that I will tend to call scopes—and explicit environments. The former is what you will use in most everyday programming, while the latter is used in more advanced techniques, which mostly add flexibility in how you can provide interfaces to users. The way that R maps names to values is the same in both settings, however, and understanding how this works can make it easier to write functions and understand advanced packages.

But let us start with a simple example. If you write an expression, such as x + y, you cannot evaluate without knowing what x and y refer to. And neither can R. If you have told R what the two variables refer to

```
x <- 2
y <- 3
x + y
```

```
## [1] 5
```

you get what you expect. R knows that x refers to 2 (because you just assigned 2 to it), and it knows that y refers to 3.

© Thomas Mailund 2023
T. Mailund, *Functional Programming in R 4*, https://doi.org/10.1007/978-1-4842-9487-1_4

You can think of this as R having a table that maps between names and values; this won't be far from the truth. If we wrote the preceding code at the global (outermost) level, the table is the "global environment" or "global scope," and we can get the table using the globalenv() function:

```
genv <- globalenv()
```

and from it, we can get the values we assigned to the variables x and y:

```
genv$x
```

```
## [1] 2
```

```
genv$y
```

```
## [1] 3
```

When we evaluated x + y, R automatically looked up the values for x and y, and it looked in the global environment because we wrote the expression in the global environment.

We can do the same thing in a more complicated way that makes the environment and evaluation explicit. You can create an expression without associated values using the quote() function:

```
expr <- quote(x + y)
```

Now, expr refers to the expression x + y, but the expression is not evaluated. It is the raw syntax for the addition. To evaluate it, we need the function eval():

```
eval(expr)
```

```
## [1] 5
```

We get the same value as before because eval() also uses the current environment to find the mapping between variable names and values, so eval(expr) is short for eval(expr, genv) in this case:

```
eval(expr, genv)
```

```
## [1] 5
```

You can, if you want, create your own environments. The new.env() function creates an empty environment that you can then write to

```
env <- new.env()
env$x <- 4
env$y <- 5
eval(expr, env)
```

```
## [1] 9
```

or the list2env() lets you translate a list into an environment:

```
eval(expr, list2env(list(x = -1, y = -2)))
```

```
## [1] -3
```

When you evaluate an expression such as x + y, using the default environment to get the values that the variables refer to, we call it *standard evaluation*. When you are explicit about the environments and use alternative environments than the default, we call it *nonstandard evaluation*. You rarely have to evaluate expressions using explicit environments—although it has its uses—but keep in mind that whenever we evaluate something where we need to know what variables refer to, some sort of lookup in a table is involved.

Environments and Functions

It gets more interesting when we add functions. With functions, we have both the global environment and the local environment for a function.

In the following code, we have two variables named x. One is a global variable that refers to a vector. The other is a function argument. Inside the function, we have an expression that refers to x. When we evaluate the function, the expression needs to figure out that the variable x is the function argument rather than the global variable before it can get to the value that the variable is referring to:

```
x <- 1:10
f <- function(x) sqrt(sum(x))
f(x**2)
```

When we call the function, we also have an expression that refers to a variable named x, but this is a different x than the variable inside the function. This x is the global variable, so when we evaluate the function call expression, R needs to figure out that x refers to the global variable and then look up the value that *this* variable is referring to.

We can clarify this by changing the names so the variables become unique. We call the global variable gx and the parameter variable px:

```
gx <- 1:10
f <- function(px) sqrt(sum(px))
f(gx**2)
```

After running this code, the global scope knows about the names gx (for the sequence 1:10) and f (for the function), but it will not know about px. Inside the function call, where we evaluate sqrt(sum(px)), we *do* know px. So what is going on?

We still have the global environment, and you can check with globalenv() that f and gx are found there. When we call f, however, we get a new environment for the function call as well—a local environment. Just as we can get the global environment using globalenv(), we can get local environments using the environment() function:

```
gx <- 1:10
f <- function(px) as.list(environment())
f(gx**2)

## $px
## [1]    1    4    9   16   25   36   49   64   81  100
```

I used as.list() to turn the environment into a list, so we can see what is inside it.

The environment() function also works in the global scope and will give you the global environment because in the global environment, the current environment *is* the global environment.

As you can see from the example, the local environment from the function contains the parameter px. Generally, the local environment of a function call will have the parameters and any variable you assign inside the function:

```
f <- function(x) {
  res <- sqrt(sum(x))
  as.list(environment())
}
x <- 1:10

f(x**2)

## $res
## [1] 19.62142
##
## $x
## [1]    1    4    9   16   25   36   49   64   81  100
```

Because I assigned to res, that variable is now also in the local environment.

Here, I also changed the argument to x, but this x will be mapped to the argument in the local environment in f rather than in the global environment, which is why a global x and a local x do not clash. When we call a function, we have two environments in play: the local environment that contains the local variables and the global environment that includes the global variables; see Figure 4-1. The code inside the function will look in the local environment to find out what values variables refer to, while global code will look in the global environment.

You might now wonder about the names sqrt() and sum() that the function f also seems to know. They aren't in the local environment. (They aren't in the global environment either; you can check with as.list(globalenv()).) So how does the function find them? We shall now see that there is one more trick to environments that handles finding variables that are not in the immediate scope and how that trick solves this problem.

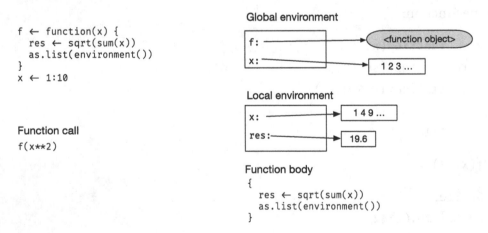

```
f ← function(x) {
  res ← sqrt(sum(x))
  as.list(environment())
}
x ← 1:10
```

Function call

`f(x**2)`

Global environment

f: ───────────────→ <function object>
x: ──────────→ 1 2 3 ...

Local environment

x: ──────────→ 1 4 9 ...
res: ─────────→ 19.6

Function body
```
{
  res ← sqrt(sum(x))
  as.list(environment())
}
```

Figure 4-1. *The local and global environments in a function call*

Environment Chains, Scope, and Function Calls

When you call a function in R, you first create an empty environment for that function. That environment is where its parameters will be stored, and any local variables the function assigns to will also go there. Whenever R needs to look up a value, it will look in this environment. If it finds the variable, you get the value in this table. If it doesn't, R doesn't just give up, however. It continues the search.

Environments are not only table but chains of tables. Each environment has a "parent" (you can use the parent.env() function to get it), and if a lookup fails for an environment, R will look in the parent instead. If it fails there, it will try the grandparent, and it will continue as long as there are environments.

Consider this code:

```
f <- function(x) {
  sqrt(sum(x + y))
}
x <- 1:10
y <- 1:10

f(x**2)
```

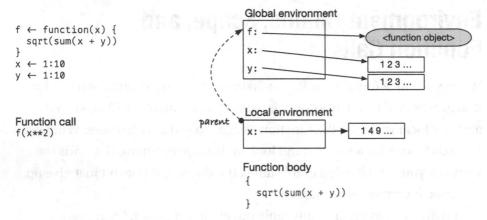

```
f ← function(x) {
  sqrt(sum(x + y))
}
x ← 1:10
y ← 1:10
```

Function call
f(x**2)

Figure 4-2. *The local and global environments are connected through a parent pointer*

[1] 20.97618

We define three variables, f, x, and y, in the global environment, where f is a function. Then we call the function, creating a local environment where f's argument x will be placed; see Figure 4-2.

The x in the local and the global environments refers to different values, and if we look for the value of x inside the function, we get the one in the local environment; see Figure 4-3. The sqrt, sum, and y names used in the function body are not defined in the local environment. If we only had environments as tables, we wouldn't be able to run this code. The parent environment, however, allows us to find nonlocal variables. When R cannot find y in the local environment, it will go to the parent environment, which is the global environment, and find it there; see Figure 4-4.

The sqrt and sum variables are also not defined in the local environment, so R will also look for them in the parent, but they are not defined in the global environment either. Although I will not look beyond the global environment in the rest of this book, the environment chain goes deeper than that. After the global environment, you will find environments that hold names from loaded packages, which is why you can use functions from packages. Once you are through them, you get to the so-called "base environment," where you find the base R functions (you can get hold of it with the baseenv() function) and then an empty environment that terminates the search. It is in this base environment we find sum and sqrt; see Figure 4-5. The mechanism is the same all the way down, so if you understand how it works between functions and the global environment, you will also understand how environments work everywhere[1].

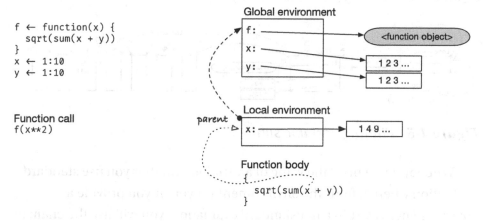

Figure 4-3. *Finding local variable x*

---

[1] <Footnote ID="Fn1"><Para ID="Par17">Packages also use the environment system to differentiate between public and private names, but not through a separate mechanism. They just use different environment chains, where we hook into the public environment while they have another environment containing the private names that we do not see.</Para></Footnote>

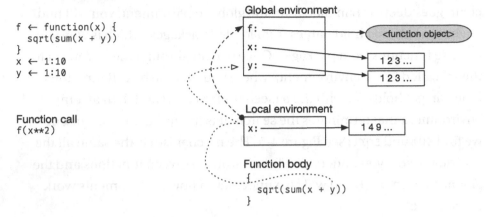

Figure 4-4. *Finding global variable y*

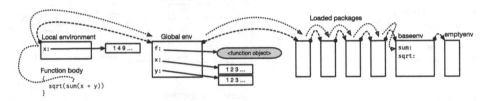

Figure 4-5. *Finding variable sum*

Whenever you need the value of a variable, whether you use standard evaluation where R finds the environment for you or you provide an environment to eval in a nonstandard evaluation, you will use the chain of parent environments to find variables that are not in the immediate scope.

Scopes, Lazy Evaluation, and Default Parameters

Knowing the rules for how variables are mapped into values also helps us understand why we can use function parameters in expressions for default parameters when defining a function, but we cannot use them when we call a function.

If we define a function with a default parameter set to an expression that refers to another parameter:

```
f <- function(x, y = 2 * x) x + y
```

we can call it like this:

```
a <- 2
f(x = a)

## [1] 6
```

but not necessarily like this:

```
f(x = a, y = 2 * x)
```

In both cases, we will create an environment for the function first, and in it, we will store the mappings from x and y to values. Except, function arguments are not passed as values but using lazy evaluation. You can think of this lazy evaluation much like the quote(x + y) expression from earlier in the chapter. It is unevaluated expressions we pass to the function, and we only evaluate them once we have to.

So, in both cases, f's environment will map x to a and y to 2 * x. We then will try to evaluate x + y, which means that we trigger evaluation of the expressions a and 2 * x, and this is where the two calls differ.

Function arguments *also* have an associated environment. In this sense, they are *not* exactly like the quote(x + y) expression. And in the first case, where x is provided but y is the default, the expression a for x knows that it should be evaluated in the global scope, where a is defined, but the default parameter y = 2 * x should be evaluated in the local environment; see Figure 4-6. So, when we try to evaluate x + y, we will evaluate the expression a in the global environment to get the value for x, and we will then evaluate the expression 2 * x in the local variable (that knows x) to get y, and that will give us the variable values we need.

In the second case, however, both x and y need to be evaluated in the global environment because we got the expressions from there. We can still evaluate a to get x, but there might not be an x in the global environment, in which case we can't evaluate 2 * x, or even worse, there is one, but it is the wrong value, so we would get a result back that isn't the one we expect.

While we evaluate parameters inside function calls, the environment we use depends on where they were provided. Default parameters will be evaluated in the local environment, see Figure 4-6, and other parameters will be evaluated in the calling scope, see Figure 4-7.

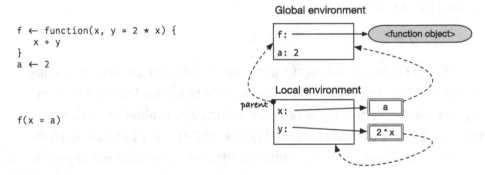

Figure 4-6. *Evaluating with a default parameter*

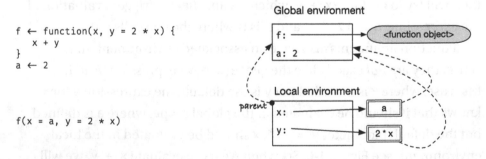

Figure 4-7. *Evaluating with an explicit argument*

76

We can exploit lazy evaluation to extract expressions rather than values and evaluate them in different environments, should we choose. A full exploration of this is beyond the scope of this book, but a short example could look like this:

```
f <- function(expr, ...) {
  expr <- substitute(expr)      # Turn argument into a plain
  expression
  env <- list2env(list(...))  # Make an env from '...'
  parent.env(env) <- parent.frame() # Get remaining args from
                                     caller's env
  eval(expr, env)               # Now evaluate the expression in
                                the new env
}

a <- 22
f(a)

## [1] 22

f(a + b, b = 13)

## [1] 35
```

You can use the substitute() function to strip an argument of its environment and only get its expression. In the function, we then use list2env to turn the ... arguments into an environment, we make the parent of this environment the calling scope (using parent.frame to get the caller's environment rather than the function's local scope), and then we evaluate the expression in the new environment. It allows us to push in extra arguments, like b = 13, and use them instead of the local environment for the evaluation.

Tricks like this are used throughout the Tidyverse ecosystem of packages, and if it is something you wish to explore further, an excellent place to start is the rlang package. It provides several high-level handles for manipulating arguments and evaluating them in alternative environments. But I will leave the topic of nonstandard evaluation here.

Nested Functions and Scopes

So far, we have only considered two environments—global and local—so it might be natural to assume that the parent of a local environment is always the global (and you might wonder why this whole mechanism is necessary in that case), but this isn't the case. It is merely an artifact of where we have defined our functions so far.

Consider this slightly weird but simple enough function:

```
f <- function() environment()
```

When we call f(), it will return its local environment, and there is nothing we haven't seen before yet. However, the environment() function takes an argument, a function, and if you call it with a function, it returns something else than the current environment. It returns the environment where the function was defined. We defined f in the global environment, so environment(f) will give us the global environment:

```
environment(f)
```

```
## <environment: R_GlobalEnv>
```

which, as should be clear by now, is different from the environment we get when we are inside the function's body:

```
f()
```

```
## <environment: 0x7fe46613ae88>
```

To expand on this a little, let us try to define a function inside f:

```
f <- function(x) {
  print(environment())  # Print the local environment
  g <- function(y) x + y
  g
}
```

Since f is still defined in the global environment, environment(f) is still R_GlobalEnv, but the function g we define inside a call to f is defined in the local environment:

```
environment(f)
```

```
## <environment: R_GlobalEnv>
```

```
g <- f(2)
```

```
## <environment: 0x7fe435b7a0a8>
```

```
environment(g)
```

```
## <environment: 0x7fe435b7a0a8>
```

As we see, the environment that we print inside the call to f() is the same as the environment associated with the function we get as the result of the function call.

It is important to note that a function's environment differs from the local environment we get when we *call* the function. The function's environment is an existing environment where we have defined the function, while the local environment is a new environment created when we call the function. If that is clear, then the rule for how R sets up the parent environment is simple enough: when you call a function, the new local environment will get the function's environment as its parent.

Let's go through the preceding example in detail. We start right after we have defined f; see Figure 4-8. At this point, we only have the global environment (ignoring the chain of parents after that) because we haven't called any function yet, and thus we haven't created any local environments. In the global environment, we have a reference to the new function—the variable f refers to the function object—and the function's environment is the global environment (where we defined it).

When we call f, we create a new environment for the function call, the parent of the new environment is the function's environment (the global environment), and we put the argument x into the local environment; see Figure 4-9.

Then, inside the function call, we define the function g; see Figure 4-10. That creates a new function object, and since it is defined inside the function call environment, that environment becomes g's environment. Since we also name the function, by assigning the function to the variable g, we also get a reference from the local environment to the function.

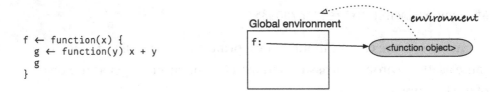

```
f ← function(x) {
  g ← function(y) x + y
  g
}
```

Figure 4-8. *After defining f*

```
f ← function(x) {
    g ← function(y) x + y
    g
}
g ← f(2)
```

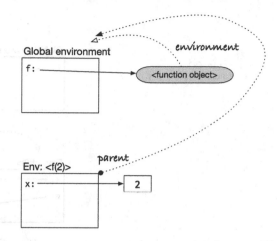

Figure 4-9. Calling f

We return the new function object from the call to f, and in this code, we assign it to a variable g in the global environment; see Figure 4-11. We didn't have to name the function object the same in the global and local environments, but in this code, we use the variable g in both environments to refer to the same object.

Usually, you can think of the local environment of a function call as disappearing when you return from a call because it is inaccessible after the function returns, but not in this case. The function we call g in the global environment has the f(2) call's environment as its function environment, so the environment is still around, which is important if we now call g (from the global environment).

81

```
f ← function(x) {
  g ← function(y) x + y
  g
}
g ← f(2)
```

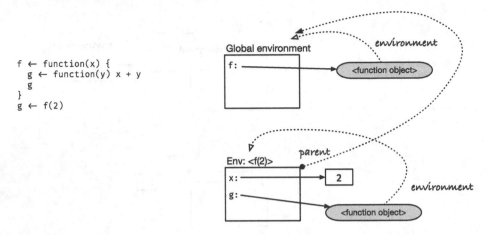

Figure 4-10. *Defining g inside a call to f*

```
f ← function(x) {
  g ← function(y) x + y
  g
}
g ← f(2)
```

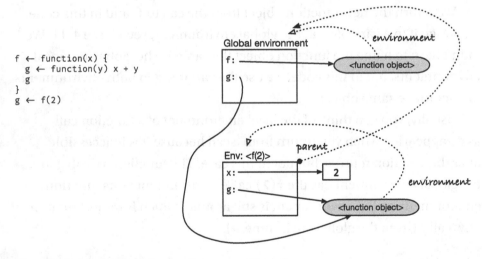

Figure 4-11. *Returning g from a call to f*

```
f ← function(x) {
  g ← function(y) x + y
  g
}
g ← f(2)
g(3)
```

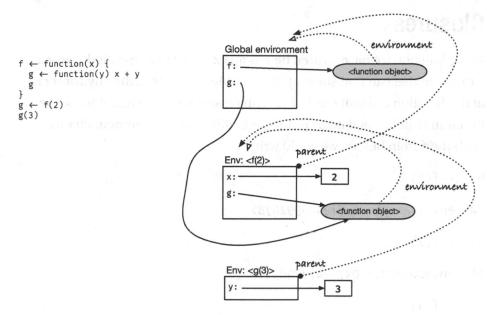

Figure 4-12. *Calling g*

g(3)

[1] 5

Let's see what happens in this call. You can follow along in Figure 4-12.

We create a new environment for the call g(3), and since g's environment is the one we created when we called f(2), that will be the parent environment. The parameter y is inserted in the new environment, so when we evaluate x + y, we can get y from there. The variable x is not in the local environment, so we must follow the parent pointer to the f(2) environment, where we find that it maps to 2.

Closures

The g function we have written here is an example of a so-called *closure*: a function that can find some of the variables it needs in the environment of the function call that created it. With closures, we can adapt the same function to different data by putting it in different environment chains. With the f from before, we could write

```
h1 <- f(1)
```

```
## <environment: 0x7fe446992678>
```

```
h2 <- f(2)
```

```
## <environment: 0x7fe4777ada20>
```

```
h3 <- f(3)
```

```
## <environment: 0x7fe477056128>
```

to get three different functions, one that adds 1 to its input, one that adds 2, and one that adds 3, all from the same code. The variable x will be found in three different environments—environments created when we called f and that map x to 1, 2, or 3, respectively.

```
sapply(1:5, h1)
```

```
## [1] 2 3 4 5 6
```

```
sapply(1:5, h2)
```

```
## [1] 3 4 5 6 7
```

```
sapply(1:5, h3)
```

```
## [1] 4 5 6 7 8
```

Closures are frequently used in functional programming because they give us a way to wrap up data together with functions so that we can separate domain information from generic code. Earlier, we called sapply() (it stands for simplifying apply) with three closures. The sapply() function calls its argument function on each element in a sequence. It doesn't know anything about what the function does, but it must be a function it can call with a single argument. By using closures, we adapted a function that does addition to a function that has already bound one of the arguments to the addition. By doing that, we adapted addition to the interface that sapply() provides.

We don't need to write functions to return closures either. Whenever you define a function, you give it access to all the variables you have in scope at the point where you define it. So if you write code such as this:

```
# Increment all elements in x by inc
inc_all <- function(x, inc) {
  sapply(x, \(a) a + inc)
}
inc_all(1:5, 3)

## [1] 4 5 6 7 8
```

you are still creating a function (in this case, we don't name it, but it is the function \(a) a + inc) that knows how much to increment by, so sapply() can use it without needing the increment amount as an extra parameter.

Of course, a vector expression

```
1:5 + 3

## [1] 4 5 6 7 8
```

would be both cleaner and more efficient than using `sapply()`, but our needs are often more complex than adding numbers. Maybe we need to check which elements in our data can be found in some database—a toy example of that could look like this:

```
## foo   qux  bar
## TRUE FALSE TRUE
```

Since `sapply()` doesn't know about databases, we need to wrap the database up in the function we provide. If we do this inside a function, `sapply()` won't have access to the `database` variable, but the function we created, `\(key) key %in% database`, does. The function will get key from `sapply()`, and it will get `database` from its scope.

Reaching Outside Your Innermost Scope

When we assign to a variable using the `<-` operator, we modify the environment at the top of the current environment chain. We modify the local environment. So what does this code do?

```
Make_counter <- function() {
    x <- 0
    count <- function() {
        x <- x + 1
        x
    }
}
counter <- make_counter()
```

The intent behind the function is to create a function, a closure, that returns an increasing number each time we call it. It is not a pure function, but it is something we could find helpful. In the depth-first numbering algorithm we wrote in the previous chapter, we had to pass along in recursive calls the current number, but if we had such a counter, we could use *it* to get the next number each time we needed it.

It doesn't work, though.

```
counter()
```

```
## [1] 1
```

```
counter()
```

```
## [1] 1
```

```
counter()
```

```
## [1] 1
```

We can unwrap the function and see what is going on. When we create the counter, we call the make_counter function, which creates an environment where x is set to zero, and then the count function, which it returns.

When we call the counter function, it knows x because it is a closure, so it can evaluate x + 1, which it then assigns to x. This is where the problem is. The x used in evaluating x + 1 is found by searching up the environment chain, but the x the function assigns to is put in the counter function's environment. Then the function returns, and that environment is gone. The next time counter is called, it is a new function instance, creating a new environment. The variable x from the make_counter function is never updated.

When you use <-, you create a new local variable if it didn't exist before. Even if the variable name is found deeper in the environment chain, it doesn't matter. The assignment always is to the local environment.

To assign to a variable deeper in the environment chain, you need to use the operator <<- instead. This operator will search through the environment chain, the same way as R does to figure out what expressions should evaluate to, and update the environment where it finds the variable (or add it to the global environment if it doesn't find it anywhere in the environment chain).

We can see what happens if we change the assignment operator in the example:

```
Make_counter <- function() {
    x <- 0
    count <- function() {
        x <<- x + 1
        x
    }
}
counter <- make_counter()
counter()

## [1] 1

counter()

## [1] 2

counter()

## [1] 3
```

This time around, when we do the assignment, we find that there is an x in the enclosing environment, the x that was initialized when we called make_counter. Hence, the assignment is to that environment instead of to the local environment. Each time we call counter, we create a new function instance environment, but all the instances are linked to the same enclosing environment, so each time we call the function, we update the same environment.

We can use this counter function together with the <<- operator to make a much simpler version of the depth_first_numbers function, where we do not need to pass data along in the recursive calls. We can create a table and a counter function in the outermost scope and simply use the counter and assign with <<- to the table:

```
depth_first_numbers <- function(tree) {
  table <- c()
  counter <- make_counter()

  traverse_tree <- function(node) {
    if (is.null(node$left) && is.null(node$right)) {
      dfn <- counter()
      node$range <- c(dfn, dfn)
      table[node$name] <<- dfn
      node

    } else {
      left <- traverse_tree(node$left)
      right <- traverse_tree(node$right)
      new_node <- make_node(node$name, left, right)
      new_node$range <- c(left$range[1], right$range[2])
      new_node
    }
  }

  new_tree <- traverse_tree(tree)
  list(tree = new_tree, table = table)
}

result <- depth_first_numbers(tree)
print_tree(result$tree)
```

```
## [1] "((A,B) ,D)"
```

```
result$table
```

```
## A B D
## 1 2 3
```

We still need to create a new tree here if we want to annotate all nodes with their depth-first-number ranges; we still cannot modify data, but we can use the variables in the outer scope inside the recursive function.

Lexical and Dynamic Scope

This rule for finding variable values, based on the environment where functions are defined, is called *lexical scoping* and is the most common standard for scopes. They are called that because you can, in principle, figure out what variables in an expression are defined where. You first check if the variables are set in the local environment, either local variables or function parameters. If not, you look at the enclosing code and check if the variable is in the environment. The enclosing code can be the global environment or a function. If it is a function and the variables are not defined, you work your way further out in the code where the function is defined. If the mapping from variables to values depended on where a function was *called* rather than where it was defined, something called *dynamic scope*, you couldn't figure out what variables variable names were referring to just from reading the code where the function is defined.

R supports both kinds of scope, with the lexical scope being the default (standard evaluation). Still, by modifying environment chains, you can get access to the calling function's scope (in nonstandard evaluation). There are cases where nonstandard evaluation gives you cleaner interfaces to your code, but you should stick to standard lexical scope in the majority of your projects, as it is by far the easiest to work with.

One common case where dynamic scope and nonstandard evaluation are worth the effort is when you need to evaluate expressions where some of your data is in variables and some in a data frame. There, you get a cleaner interface if you can use the data frame variables as if they were standard variables. So, I will give you an example of how you can achieve that.

We will write a function that takes an expression and a data frame as input, and it will evaluate the expression in an environment where it first looks for variables in the data frame. If it cannot find it there, it will look in the caller's (not the function's) environment.

It looks like this:

```
df_eval <- function(expr, df = list()) {
  x <- substitute(expr) # strip expr of env; now just
  quoted expr
  env <- list2env(df, parent = parent.frame())
  eval(x, env)
}
```

We use the substitute() function to strip expr of its environment. It turns it into a raw expression, just as what we can create with quote(). I store it in a variable x to make a point in a little bit; normally, I would probably call it expr.

Anyway, the next thing we do is create a new environment from the data frame. Data frames are also lists, so list2env() will create an environment where each variable in the data frame is stored as an environment variable. The parent of the new environment is parent.frame(), which is the caller's environment. Setting it up this way puts the data frame first, so we will pick variables we can find there before we look in the parent frame. If we don't see a variable in the data frame, we will look in the caller's environment. Finally, we evaluate x in the new environment.

Let's set some data up for an experiment:

```
x <- 1:3
y <- "foo"
df <- data.frame(y = 2:4, z = 3:5)
```

We have an x and a y in the caller's environment and y and z in a data frame. We want the function to pick this x rather than the one inside df_eval, and if we call df_eval with df as the data frame, we shouldn't pick the variable y but rather the y from the data frame.

Let's check it out. First, call it with just x:

```
df_eval(x)
```

```
## [1] 1 2 3
```

We didn't provide a data frame, so we got the default, but the point of this call was to show that we picked the x in the global environment and not the x inside the function.

Now, let's see if it will pick the y from the data frame over the variable here:

```
df_eval(y+z, df)
```

```
## [1] 5 7 9
```

Yup, it works as expected.

Several built-in functions in R do nonstandard evaluation in this way—putting data frames into the current environment when evaluating an expression—and it is a fair way to exploit the environment mechanism. Don't go overboard, though.

CHAPTER 5

Higher-Order Functions

The term *higher-order functions* refers to functions that either take functions as arguments or return functions. The functions we used to create closures in the previous chapter are thus higher-order functions. Higher-order functions are frequently used in R instead of looping control structures, and we will cover how you can do this in general in the next chapter. I will just give you a quick example here before moving on to more interesting things we can do with functions working on functions.

The function `sapply`, which we saw in the last chapter, lets you call a function for all elements in a list or vector. You should mainly use this for interactive in R because it is a little unsafe. It tries to guess at which type of output you want, based on what the input and the function you give it does, and there are safer alternatives, `vapply` and `lapply`, where the output is always a predefined type or always a list, respectively.

In any case, if you want to evaluate a function for all elements in a vector, you can write code like this:

```
sapply(1:4, sqrt)
```

```
## [1] 1.000000 1.414214 1.732051 2.000000
```

© Thomas Mailund 2023
T. Mailund, *Functional Programming in R 4*, https://doi.org/10.1007/978-1-4842-9487-1_5

This evaluates sqrt on all the elements in the vector 1:4 and gives you the result. It is an analog to the vectorized expression, and the vectorized version is probably always preferable if your expressions can be vectorized. The vector expression is easier to read and usually much faster if it involves calling built-in functions:

```
sqrt(1:4)
```

You can use sapply to evaluate a function on all elements in a sequence when the function you want to call is not vectorized, however, and in fact, the Vectorize function we saw in the first chapter is implemented using sapply's cousin, lapply.

We could implement our own version like this:

```
myapply <- function(x, f) {
  result <- x
  for (i in seq_along(x))
    result[i] <- f(x[i])
  result
}

myapply(1:4, sqrt)

## [1] 1.000000 1.414214 1.732051 2.000000
```

Here, I create a result vector of the right length just by copying x. The assignments into this vector might create copies. The first is guaranteed to because we are changing a vector, which R avoids by making a copy. Later assignments might do it again to convert the type of the results. Still, it is reasonably simple to see how it works, and if the input and output have the same type, it is running in linear time (in the number of function calls to f which of course can have any runtime complexity).

Using a function like sapply or myapply, or any of their cousins, lets us replace with a single function call a loop, where all kinds of nastiness can happen with assignments to local variables that we do not necessarily want. We just need to wrap the body of the loop in another function we can give to the apply function.

Closures can be particularly useful in combination with apply functions if we need to pass some information along to the function. Let us, for example, consider a situation where we want to scale the element in a vector. We wrote such a function in the first chapter:

```
rescale <- function(x) {
  m <- mean(x)
  s <- sd(x)
  (x - m) / s
}
rescale(1:4)
```

```
## [1] -1.1618950 -0.3872983  0.3872983  1.1618950
```

This was written using vector expressions, which is the right thing to do, but let us see what we can do with an apply function. Obviously, we still need to compute m and s and then a function for computing (x - m) / s:

```
rescale <- function(x) {
  m <- mean(x)
  s <- sd(x)
  f <- function(y) (y - m) / s
  myapply(x, f)
}
rescale(1:4)
```

```
## [1] -1.1618950 -0.3872983  0.3872983  1.1618950
```

There is really no need to give the function a name and then pass it along; we can also just write

```
rescale <- function(x) {
  m <- mean(x)
  s <- sd(x)
  myapply(x, \(y) (y - m) / s)
}
rescale(1:4)
```

```
## [1] -1.1618950 -0.3872983  0.3872983  1.1618950
```

The function we pass to myapply, \(y) ..., knows the environment in which it was created, so it knows m and s and can use these variables when it is being called from myapply.

Currying

It is not unusual to have a function of two arguments where you want to bind one of them and return a function that takes, as a parameter, the second argument. For example, if we want to use the function

```
f <- function(x, y) x + y
```

we might want to use it to add 2 to each element in a sequence using myapply. Once again, I stress that this example is just to show you a general technique, and you should never do these things when you can solve a problem with vector expressions. Still, let us for a second pretend that we don't have vector expressions. Then we would need to create a function for one of the parameters, say y, and then when called evaluate f(2,y).

We could write it like this, obviously:

```
g <- function(y) f(2, y)
```

```
myapply(1:4, g)
```

```
## [1] 3 4 5 6
```

or shorter as

```
myapply(1:4, \(y) f(2, y))
```

```
## [1] 3 4 5 6
```

which would suffice if we only ever needed to add 2 to all elements in a sequence. If we wanted a more general solution, we would want a function to create the function we need, a closure that remembers x and can be called with y. Such a function is only slightly more complicated to write; we simply need a function that returns a function like this:

```
h <- function(x) \(y) f(x, y)
myapply(1:4, h(2))
```

```
## [1] 3 4 5 6
```

The functions f and h eventually do the same thing, the only difference is in how we provide parameters to them. Function f needs both parameters at once, while function h takes one parameter at a time:

```
f(2, 2)
```

```
## [1] 4
```

```
h(2)(2)
```

```
## [1] 4
```

A function such as h, one that takes a sequence of parameters not in a single function call but through a sequence of function calls, each taking a single parameter and returning a new function, is known as a *curried*

function. What we did to transform f into h is called *currying* f. The names
refer to the logician Haskell Curry, from whom we also get the name of the
functional programming language Haskell.

The transformation we did from f to h was manual, but we can write
functions that transform functions: functions that take a function as input
and return another function. We can thus write a general function for
currying a function—another high-level function. A function for currying
functions of two parameters can be written like this:

```
curry2 <- function(f) \(x) \(y) f(x, y)
```

The argument f is the function we want to curry, and the return value
is the function

```
\(x) \(y) f(x, y)
```

that needs to be called first with parameter x and then with parameter y,
and then it will return the value f(x, y). The names of the variables do
not matter here, they are just names and need not have anything to do with
the names of the variables that f actually takes.

Using this function, we can automatically create h from f:

```
h <- curry2(f)
f(2, 3)

## [1] 5

h(2)(3)

## [1] 5
```

Since + is just a function in R, we can also simply use *it* instead of
writing the function f first:

```
h <- curry2(`+`)
h(2)(3)
```

```
## [1] 5
```

and thus write the code that adds 2 to all elements in a sequence like this:

```
myapply(1:4, curry2(`+`)(2))
```

```
## [1] 3 4 5 6
```

Whether you find this clever or too terse to be easily understood is a matter of taste. It is clearly not as elegant as vector expressions, but once you are familiar with what currying does, it is not difficult to parse either. That being said, I would prefer any day of the week, as I find this version easier to read. But we will continue with currying a little bit further to explore it. Notice, however, that all the different approaches are doing the same thing: translating a binary + into a single function, by binding the first argument.

```
myapply(1:4, \(y) 2 + y)
```

```
## [1] 3 4 5 6
```

The function we wrote for currying only works on functions that take exactly two arguments. We explicitly created a function that returns a function that returns the final value, so the curried version has to work on functions with two arguments. But functions are data that we can examine in R, so we can create a general version that can handle functions of any number of arguments. We simply need to know the number of arguments the function takes and then create a sequence of functions for taking each parameter.

The full implementation is shown as follows, and I will explain it in detail after the function listing:

```
curry <- function(f) {
  n <- length(formals(f))
  if (n == 1) return(f) # no currying needed

  arguments <- vector("list", length = n)
```

```
last <- function(x) {
  arguments[n] <<- x
  do.call(f, arguments)
}
make_i <- function(i, continuation) {
  force(i) ; force(continuation)
  function(x) {
    arguments[i] <<- x
    continuation
  }
}

continuation <- last
for (i in seq(n-1, 1)) {
  continuation <- make_i(i, continuation)
}
continuation
}
```

First, we get the number of arguments that function f takes:

```
n <- length(formals(f))
```

We can get these arguments using the `formals` function. It returns what is called a pair-list, which is essentially a linked list similar to the one we saw in chapter 3 and is used internally in R but not in actual R programming. You can treat it as a list, and it behaves the same way except for some runtime performance differences. We just need to know the length of the list.

We just return if f only takes a single argument. Then it is already as curried as it can get. Otherwise, we create a table in which we will store variables when the chain of functions is called:

```
arguments <- vector("list", length = n)
```

- We need to collect the arguments that are passed to
  the individual functions we create. We cannot simply
  use parameter arguments x and y as we did in curry2
  because we do not know how many arguments we
  would need before we have examined the input
  function, f. In any case, we would need to create
  names dynamically to make sure they don't clash. Just
  saving the arguments in a list is simpler, and since it is
  a list, we can put any kind of values that are passed as
  arguments in it.

Now we need to create the actual function we should return. We
do this in steps. The final function we create should call f with all the
arguments. It takes the last argument as input, so we need to store that in
arguments—and since this means modifying a list outside of the scope of
the actual function, we need the <<- assignment operator for that. To call
f with a list of its arguments, we need to use the function do.call. It lets
us specify the arguments to the function in a list instead of giving them
directly as comma-separated arguments.

```
last <- function(x) {
  arguments[n] <<- x
  do.call(f, arguments)
}
```

Each of the other functions needs to store an argument as well, so
they will need to know the corresponding index, and then they should
return the next function in the curried chain. We can create such functions
like this:

```
make_i <- function(i, continuation) {
  force(i) ; force(continuation)
```

```
function(x) {
  arguments[i] <<- x
  continuation
  }
}
```

The parameter i is the index, which we use to assign a value to an argument, and the parameter continuation is the function that still remains to be called before the final result can be returned from function last. It is the continuation of the curried function. We need to evaluate both parameters inside make_i before we return the function. Otherwise, we run into the lazy evaluation problem where, when we eventually call the function, values of variables might have changed since we created the function. We do this by calling force on the arguments.

We now simply need to bind it all together. We do this in reverse order, so we always have the continuation we need when we create the next function. The first continuation is the last function. It is the last function that should be called, and it will return the desired result of the entire curried chain. Each call to make_i will return a new continuation that we provide to the next function in the chain (in reverse order):

```
continuation <- last
for (i in seq(n-1, 1)) {
  continuation <- make_i(i, continuation)
}
```

The final continuation we create is the curried function, so that is what we return at the end of curry.

Now we can use this curry function to translate any function into a curried version:

```
f <- function(x, y, z) x + 2*y + 3*z
f(1, 2, 3)
```

```
## [1] 14
```

```
curry(f)(1)(2)(3)
```

```
## [1] 14
```

It is not *quite* the same semantics as calling f directly; we are evaluating each expression when we assign it to the `arguments` table, so lazy evaluation isn't in play here. To write a function that can deal with the lazy evaluation of the parameters requires a lot of mucking about with environments and expressions that is beyond the scope of this book. Aside from that, though, we have written a general function for translating normal functions into their curried form.

It is *much* harder to make a transformation in the other direction automatically. If we get a function, we cannot see how many times we would need to call it to get a value, if that is even independent of the parameters we give it, so there is no way to figure out how many parameters we should get for the uncurried version of a curried function.

The `curry` function isn't completely general. We cannot deal with default arguments—all arguments must be provided in the curried version—and we cannot create a function where some arguments are fixed, and others are not. The curried version always needs to take the arguments in the exact order the original function takes them.

A Parameter Binding Function

We already have all the tools we need to write a function that binds a set of parameters for a function and return another function where we can give the remaining parameters and get a value:

```
bind_parameters <- function(f, ...) {
  remembered <- list(...)
  function(...) {
```

```
    new <- list(...)
    do.call(f, c(remembered, new))
  }
}

f <- function(x, y, z, w = 4) x + 2*y + 3*z + 4*w

f(1, 2, 3, 4)

## [1] 30

g <- bind_parameters(f, y = 2)
g(x = 1, z = 3)

## [1] 30

h <- bind_parameters(f, y = 1, w = 1)
f(2, 1, 3, 1)

## [1] 17

h(x = 2, z = 3)

## [1] 17
```

We get the parameters from the first function call and save them in a list, and then we return a closure that can take the remaining parameters, turn them into a list, combine the remembered and the new parameters, and call function f using do.call.

All the building blocks we have seen before, we are just combining them to translate one function into another.

Using list here to remember the parameters from ... means that we are evaluating the parameters. We are explicitly turning off lazy evaluation in this function. It is possible to keep the lazy evaluation semantics as well, but it requires more work. We would need to use the eval(substitu te(alist(...))) trick to get the unevaluated parameters into a list—we saw this trick in the first chapter—but that would give us raw expressions in the lists, and we would need to be careful to evaluate these in the right environment chain to make it work. I leave this as an exercise to the reader, or you can look at the partial function from the pryr package to see how it is done.

Such partial binding functions aren't used that often in R. It is just as easy to write closures to bind parameters and those are usually easier to read, so use partial bindings with caution.

Continuation-Passing Style

The trick we used to create curry involved creating a chain of functions where each function returns the next function that should be called, the *continuation*. This idea of having the remainder of a computation as a function you can eventually call can be used in many other problems.

Consider the simple task of adding all elements in a list. We can write a function for doing this in the following three ways:

```
my_sum_direct <- function(lst) {
  if (is_empty(lst)) 0
  else first(lst) + my_sum_direct(rest(lst))
}
my_sum_acc <- function(lst, acc = 0) {
  if (is_empty(lst)) acc
  else my_sum_acc(rest(lst), first(lst) + acc)
}
my_sum_cont <- function(lst, cont = identity) {
  if (is_empty(lst)) cont(0)
  else my_sum_cont(rest(lst),
                   function(acc) cont(first(lst) + acc))
}
```

The first function handles the computation in an obvious way by adding the current element to the result of the recursive call. The second function uses an accumulator to make a tail-recursive version, where the accumulator carries a partial sum along with the recursion. The third version also gives us a tail-recursive function but in this case via a continuation function. This function works as the accumulator in the second function; it just wraps the computation inside a function that is passed along in the recursive call.

Here, the continuation captures the partial sum moving down the recursion—the same job as the accumulator has in the second function—but expressed as an as-yet not evaluated function. This function will eventually be called by the sum of values for the rest of the recursion, so the job at this place in the recursion is simply to take the value it will eventually be provided, add the current value, and then call the continuation it was passed earlier to complete the computation.

For something as simple as adding the numbers in a list, continuation passing is of course overkill. If you need tail-recursion, the accumulator version is simpler and faster, and in any case, you are just replacing recursion going down the vector with function calls in the continuation moving up again (but see later for a solution to this problem). Still, seeing the three approaches to recursion—direct, accumulator, and continuation passing—in a trivial example makes it easier to see how they work and how they differ.

A common use of continuations is to translate nontail-recursive functions into tail-recursive. As an example, we return to the function from Chapter 3 that we used to compute the size of a tree. In that solution, we needed to handle internal nodes by first calling recursively on the left subtree and then the right subtree, to get the sizes of these, and then combining them and adding one for the internal node. Because we needed the results from two recursive calls, we couldn't directly make the function tail-recursive. Using continuations, we can.

The trick is to pass a continuation along that is used to wrap one of the recursions, while we can handle the other recursions in a tail-recursive call. The solution looks like this:

```
size_of_tree <- function(node, continuation = identity) {
  if (is.null(node$left) && is.null(node$right)) {
    # A leaf, of size 1.
    # Tell the continuation to compute the rest from
    #   that value.
    continuation(1)
  } else {
    # Make a continuation that will be called with the size of
    #   the left tree
    left_continuation <- function(left_result) {
      # When we have the size of the left tree, create a
      #   continuation that
      # combines left and right tree (and give it to the
      #   continuation)
      right_continuation <- function(right_result) {
        continuation(left_result + right_result + 1)
      }

      # Compute the size of the right tree
      size_of_tree(node$right, right_continuation)
    }

    # Compute the size of the left tree
    size_of_tree(node$left, left_continuation)
  }
}

tree <- make_node("root",
```

```
                make_node("C", make_node("A"),
                               make_node("B")),
                make_node("D"))
```

```
size_of_tree(tree)
```

```
## [1] 5
```

The function takes a continuation along in its call, and this function is responsible for computing "the rest of what needs to be done." If the node we are looking at is a leaf, we call it with 1, because a leaf has size one, and then it will do whatever computation is needed to compute the size of the tree we have seen earlier and wrapped in the continuation parameter.

The default continuation is the identity function:

```
function(x) x
```

so if we just call the function with a leaf, we will get 1 as the value. But we modify the continuation when we see an internal node to wrap some of the computation we cannot do yet because we do not have the full information for what we need to compute.

For internal nodes, we do this:

```
# Make a continuation that will be called with the size of the
left tree
left_continuation <- function(left_result) {
  # When we have the size of the left tree, create a
    continuation that
  # combines left and right tree (and give it to the
    continuation)
  right_continuation <- function(right_result) {
    continuation(left_result + right_result + 1)
  }

  # Compute the size of the right tree
```

```
    size_of_tree(node$right, right_continuation)
}

# Compute the size of the left tree
size_of_tree(node$left, left_continuation)
```

We create a continuation that, if we give it the size of the left subtree, can compute the size of the full tree. When it is called, it gets the size of the left subtree as its argument, but it needs to compute the size of the right subtree itself. For that, it needs a continuation that will get the size of the right tree, and when *that* function is called, we can return the size of the inner node: the size of the left tree plus the size of the right tree plus one. It returns it by calling the continuation, which will then handle whatever has to happen as we return from the recursion.

The `left_continuation` calls a recursion on the right tree with this `right_continuation`, thus getting the size of the right tree into the `right_continuation` function. But before `left_continuation` is called, we call `size_of_tree(node$left, left_continuation)` to get the size of the left tree. When we have traversed the left tree, `left_continuation` is called with its size.

Because it is tail-recursive, we can replace the recursive calls with a loop. This time around, we need to remember to `force` the evaluation of the continuation when we create the new continuation because when we loop we are modifying local parameters. Otherwise, it looks like you would expect from the general pattern for translating tail-recursive functions into looping functions.

```
size_of_tree <- function(node, continuation = identity) {
  repeat {
    if (is.null(node$left) && is.null(node$right)) {
      return(continuation(1))
    }
    new_continuation <- function(continuation) {
```

```
      force(continuation)
      function(left_result) {
        size_of_tree(
          node$right,
          \(right_result) continuation(left_result + right_
          result + 1)
        )
      }
    }

    # simulated recursive call
    node <- node$left
    continuation <- new continuation(continuation)
  }
}

size_of_tree(tree)
```

```
## [1] 5
```

There is a catch, though. We avoid deep recursions to the left, but the continuation we create is going to call functions just as deep as we would earlier do the recursion. The recursive calls to the right are still function calls—we need a second continuation there, and we cannot yet overwrite the left continuation. Furthermore, each time we would usually call recursively, we are wrapping a function inside another, and when these need to be evaluated, we still have a deep number of function calls.

It is still possible to translate functions such as these into pure loops, but it requires that *all* tail-calls (functions where we immediately return their result) are optimized. Some programming languages implement this, it is typical for all pure programming languages, but R does not. And it is not easy to rewrite this to a looping function ourselves either, unfortunately.

However, there is a trick to get around this, using closures. It won't give us the performance boost of using a loop instead of recursions, it will actually be slightly slower, but it will let us write functions with more than one recursion without having too deep recursive calls. If you have an algorithm where you need recursion, or just where recursion gives you a simpler implementation, and you don't desperately need high performance, you can use this general trick.

Thunks and Trampolines

There are two pieces to the solution of too deep recursions. The first is something called a "thunk." It is simply a function that takes no arguments and returns a value. It is used to wrap up a little bit of computation that you can evaluate later. We can turn a function, with its arguments, into a thunk like this:

```
# A function we can call directly as e.g. f(1, 2)
f <- function(x, y) x + y

# thunk will call f(1, 2)
thunk <- \() f(1, 2)

f(1, 2)

## [1] 3

thunk()

## [1] 3
```

We wrap a call to f, f(1, 2), in a function that doesn't take any arguments, \() f(1, 2), so without invoking f we have created a function, thunk, that *if* we call it will evaluate f(1, 2). It is a bit like the lazy evaluation of function arguments.

If you are in an environment where f might bind to other values later, you can go a bit further. You don't want \() f(1, 2) because that will call the current f, whatever that is, when you call thunk(), but you can put f in an environment where it doesn't change with something like this:

```
make_thunk <- function(f, ...) {
  # Make sure the variables don't change after we return
  force(f)
  params <- list(...)
  # Then return the thunk
  \() do.call(f, params)
}

g <- make_thunk(f, 1, 2)
g()
## [1] 3
```

By calling force(f), you make sure that the f in the thunk's environment stays the same, and by evaluating the ... parameter immediately (by putting it in a list), you ensure that the variables are bound to the values they have when you create the thunk, rather than what values they might have when you call it.

The first construction is simpler, but if you have nonpure functions, and variables can change, the second is safer.

If you are wondering why such functions are called "thunks," here is what the Hacker's Dictionary has to say:

> Historical note: There are a couple of onomatopoeic myths circulating about the origin of this term. The most common is that it is the sound made by data hitting the stack; another holds that the sound is

that of the data hitting an accumulator. Yet another holds that it is the sound of the expression being unfrozen at argument-evaluation time. In fact, according to the inventors, it was coined after they realized (in the wee hours after hours of discussion) that the type of an argument in Algol-60 could be figured out in advance with a little compile-time thought, simplifying the evaluation machinery. In other words, it had "already been thought of"; thus it was christened a thunk, which is "the past tense of 'think' at two in the morning."

We are going to wrap recursive calls into thunks where each thunk takes one step in a recursion. Each thunk evaluates one step and returns a new thunk that will evaluate the next step and so on until a thunk eventually returns a value. The term for such evaluations is a "trampoline," and the imagery is that each thunk bounces on the trampoline, evaluates one step, and lands on the trampoline again as the next thunk.

A trampoline is just a function that keeps evaluating thunks until it gets a value, and the implementation looks like this:

```
trampoline <- function(thunk) {
  while (is.function(thunk)) thunk <- thunk()
  thunk
}
```

To see how thunks and trampolines can be combined to avoid recursion, we will first consider the simpler case of calculating the factorial of a number instead of the size of a tree.

We wrote the recursive factorial function in Chapter 3, and the nontail-recursive version looked like this:

```
factorial <- function(n) {
  if (n == 1) 1
  else n * factorial(n - 1)
}
```

The tail-recursive version, using an accumulator, looked like this:

```
factorial <- function(n, acc = 1) {
  if (n == 1) acc
  else factorial(n - 1, acc * n)
}
```

To get the thunk-trampoline version, we are first going to rewrite this using continuation passing. This is mostly just turning the accumulator in the tail-recursive version into a continuation for computing the final result:

```
cp_factorial <- function(n, continuation = identity) {
  if (n == 1) {
    continuation(1)
  } else {
    cp_factorial(n - 1, \(result) continuation(result * n))
  }
}
```

```
factorial(10)
```

```
## [1] 3628800
```

```
cp_factorial(10)
```

```
## [1] 3628800
```

This function does the same as the accumulator version, and because there is no tail-recursion optimization, it will call cp_factorial all the way down from n to 1, and then it will evaluate continuation functions just as many times. We can get it to work for n maybe up to a thousand or so, but after that, we hit the recursion stack limit. Before we reach that limit, the number will be too large to represent as floating-point numbers in R anyway, but that is not the point; the point is that the number of recursive calls can get too large for us to handle.

So instead of calling recursively, we want each "recursive" call to create a thunk instead. This will create a thunk that does the next step and returns a thunk for the step after that, but it will not call the next step, so no recursion. We need such thunks both for the recursions and the continuations. The implementation is simple; we just replace the recursions with calls to make_thunk:

```
thunk_factorial <- function(n, continuation = identity) {
  if (n == 1) {
    continuation(1)
  } else {
    # The new continuation is a function that returns a thunk.
    # The thunk will run the next step of the computation by
    # calling the continuation
    new_continuation <- \(result) \() continuation(n * result)

    # We don't call the factorial recursion yet, we just
    return a
    # thunk that is ready to take the first step of the
    computation
    \() thunk_factorial(n - 1, new_continuation)
  }
}
```

Calling this function with 1 directly gives us a value:

```
thunk_factorial(1)
```

```
## [1] 1
```

Calling it with 2 creates a thunk. We need to call this thunk to move down the recursion to the base case; this will give us a thunk for the continuation there, and we need to evaluate that thunk to get the value:

```
# Takes us one step down the recursion, but not up again
thunk_factorial(2)()
```

```
## \() continuation(n * result)
## <bytecode: 0x7fe42629e860>
## <environment: 0x7fe4263bcb38>
```

```
# The next call will take us up to a result
thunk_factorial(2)()()
```

```
## [1] 2
```

For each additional step in the recursion, we thus get two more thunks, one for going down the recursion and the next for evaluating the thunk, but, eventually, we will have evaluated all the thunks and will get a value:

```
thunk_factorial(3)()()()()
```

```
## [1] 6
```

```
thunk_factorial(4)()()()()()()
```

```
## [1] 24
```

```
thunk_factorial(5)()()()()()()()()
```

```
## [1] 120
```

Of course, we don't want to call all these thunks explicitly; that is what the trampoline is for:

```
trampoline(thunk_factorial(100))
```

```
## [1] 9.332622e+157
```

We can write another higher-order function for translating such a thunkenized function into one that uses the trampoline to do the calculation like this:

```
make_trampoline <- function(f) \(...) trampoline(f(...))
factorial <- make_trampoline(thunk_factorial)
factorial(100)
```

```
## [1] 9.332622e+157
```

For computing the size of a tree, we just do exactly the same thing. It doesn't matter that the continuation we use here does something more complex—it calls the depth-first traversal on the right subtree instead of just computing an expression directly—because it is just a continuation, and we just need to wrap it up as a thunk:

```
thunk_size <- function(node, continuation = identity) {
  if (is.null(node$left) && is.null(node$right)) {
    continuation(1)
  } else {
    left_continuation <- function(left_result) {
      # Right continuation gives us a thunk for returning with
      # the size of the current tree (left + right + 1).
      right_continuation <- function(right_result)
        \() continuation(left_result + right_result + 1)

      # Return thunk for recursing right
      \() thunk_size(node$right, right_continuation)
    }
```

```
  # Return thunk for recursing left
  \() thunk_size(node$left, left_continuation)
 }
}

size_of_tree <- make_trampoline(thunk_size)
size_of_tree(tree)
```

```
## [1] 5
```

The way we make the trampoline version is *exactly* the same as what we did for the factorial function. We make a continuation-passing version of the recursion, then we translate the direct recursive calls into thunks, and we make our continuations return thunks. Using the trampoline, we never run into problems with hitting the call stack limit; we never call recursively, we just create thunks on the fly whenever we would otherwise need to call a function.

## CHAPTER 6

Filter, Map, and Reduce

The last chapter covered some pieces of functional programming that can be hard to wrap your head around, but this chapter will be much simpler. We will look at three general methods used in functional programming instead of loops and instead of explicitly writing recursive functions. They are really three different patterns for computing on sequences, and they come in different flavors with different functions, but just these three let you do almost anything you would otherwise do with loops.

Note the *almost* earlier. These three functions do not replace *everything* you can do with loops. You can replace for-loops, where you already know how much you are looping over, but they cannot substitute while- and repeat-loops. Still, by far the most loops you write in R are for-loops, and in general, you can use these functions to replace those.

The functions, or patterns, are Filter, Map, and Reduce. The first takes a sequence and a predicate, a function that returns a boolean value, and it returns a sequence where all elements where the predicate was true are included, and the rest are removed. The second, Map, evaluates a function on each item in a sequence and returns a sequence with the results of evaluating the function. It is similar to the sapply function we briefly saw in the previous chapter. The last, Reduce, takes a sequence and a function and evaluates the function repeatedly to reduce the sequence to a single value. This pattern is also called "fold" in some programming languages.

© Thomas Mailund 2023

T. Mailund, *Functional Programming in R 4*, https://doi.org/10.1007/978-1-4842-9487-1_6

The General Sequence Object in R Is a List

Sequences come in essentially two flavors in R, vectors and lists. Vectors can only contain basic types, and all elements in a vector must have the same type.

Lists can contain a sequence of any type, and the elements in a list can have different types. Lists are thus more general than vectors and are often the building blocks of data structures such as the "next lists" and the trees we have used earlier in the book.

It, therefore, comes as no surprise that general functions for working on sequences would work on lists. The three functions, `Filter`, `Map`, and `Reduce`, are also happy to take vectors, but they are treated as if you explicitly converted them to lists first. The `Reduce` function returns a value (i.e., not a sequence) of a type that depends on its input, while `Filter` and `Map` both return sequences in the form of lists.

From a programming perspective, it is just as easy to work with lists as it is to work with vectors, but some functions do expect vectors—plotting functions and functions for manipulating data frames, for example—so sometimes you will have to translate a list from `Filter` or `Map` into a vector. You can do this with the function `unlist`. This function will convert a list into a vector when possible, that is, when all elements are of the same basic type, and otherwise will just give you the list back. I will use `unlist` in many examples in this chapter just because it makes the output nicer to look at, but in most programs, I do not bother doing so until I really need a vector. A list is just as good for storing sequences.

It is just that

```
list(1, 2, 3, 4)
```

```
## [[1]]
## [1] 1
##
## [[2]]
```

```
## [1] 2
##
## [[3]]
## [1] 3
##
## [[4]]
## [1] 4
```

gives us much longer output listings to put in the book than

```
1:4
```

```
## [1] 1 2 3 4
```

If you follow along in front of your computer, you can try to see the results with and without unlist to get a feeling for the differences.

You rarely need to convert sequences the other way, from vectors to lists. Functions that work on lists usually also work on vectors, but if you want to, you should use the as.list function and not the list function. The former gives you a list with one element per element in the vector:

```
as.list(1:4)
```

```
## [[1]]
## [1] 1
##
## [[2]]
## [1] 2
##
## [[3]]
## [1] 3
##
## [[4]]
## [1] 4
```

whereas the latter gives you a list with a single element that contains the vector:

```
list(1:4)
```

```
## [[1] ]
## [1]  1  2  3  4
```

Filtering Sequences

The Filter function is the simplest of the three main functions we cover in this chapter. It simply selects a subset of a sequence based on a predicate. A predicate is a function that returns a single boolean value, and Filter will return a list of elements where the predicate returns TRUE and discard the elements where the predicate returns FALSE.

```
is_even <- \(x) x %% 2 == 0
unlist(Filter(is_even, 1:10))
```

```
## [1]  2  4  6  8 10
```

The function is often used together with closures so the predicate can depend on local variables:

```
larger_than <- \(x) \(y) y > x
unlist(Filter(larger_than(5), 1:10))
```

```
## [1]  6  7  8  9 10
```

Not that you would write code like the preceding example in practice, since a simpler version will do:

```
unlist(Filter(\(y) y > 5, 1:10))
```

```
## [1]  6  7  8  9 10
```

but closures do work and can be very useful in more complicated situations.

Here, we have used a vector as input to `Filter`, but any list will do, and we do not need to limit it to sequences of the same type:

```
s <- list(a = 1:10,                    # A vector
          b = list(1,2,3,4,5,6),       # A list
          c = y ~ x1 + x2 + x3,        # A formula
          d = vector("numeric"))       # An empty vector
Filter(function(x) length(x) > 5, s)
```

```
## $a
##  [1]  1  2  3  4  5  6  7  8  9 10
##
## $b
## $b[[1]]
## [1] 1
##
## $b[[2]]
## [1] 2
##
## $b[[3]]
## [1] 3
##
## $b[[4]]
## [1] 4
##
## $b[[5]]
## [1] 5
##
## $b[[6]]
## [1] 6
```

When printed, the result isn't pretty, but we can't solve that with unlist in this case. Using unlist, we *would* get a vector, but not one remotely reflecting the structure of the result; the vector a and list b would be flattened into a single vector.

Mapping over Sequences

The Map function evaluates a function for each element in a list and returns a list with the results:

```
unlist(Map(is_even, 1:5))
```

```
## [1] FALSE  TRUE FALSE  TRUE FALSE
```

As with Filter, Map is often combined with closures:

```
add <- function(x) function(y) x + y
unlist(Map(add(2), 1:5))
```

```
## [1] 3 4 5 6 7
```

```
unlist(Map(add(3), 1:5))
```

```
## [1] 4 5 6 7 8
```

and can be applied on lists of different types:

```
s <- list(a = 1:10, b = list(1,2,3,4,5,6),
          c = y ~ x1 + x2 + x3, d = vector("numeric"))
unlist(Map(length, s))
```

```
##  a  b  c  d
## 10  6  3  0
```

Map can be applied to more than one sequence if the function you provide it takes a number of parameters that matches the number of sequences:

```
unlist(Map(`+`, 1:5, 1:5))
```

```
## [1]  2  4  6  8 10
```

In this example, we use the function +, which takes two arguments, and we give the Map function two sequences, so the result is the component-wise addition.

You can pass along parameters to a Map call, either directly as a named parameter

```
x <- 1:10
y <- c(NA, x)
s <- list(x = x, y = y)
unlist(Map(mean, s))
```

```
##   x  y
## 5.5 NA
```

```
unlist(Map(mean, s, na.rm = TRUE))
```

```
##   x   y
## 5.5 5.5
```

or as a list provided to the MoreArgs parameter:

```
unlist(Map(mean, s, MoreArgs = list(na.rm = TRUE)))
```

```
##   x   y
## 5.5 5.5
```

For a single value, the two approaches work the same, but their semantics is slightly different, which comes into play when providing arguments that are sequences. Providing a named argument directly to Map works just as providing an unnamed argument (except that you can pick a specific variable by name instead of by position), so Map assumes that you want to apply your function to every element of the argument. The reason this works with a single argument is that, as R generally does, the shorter sequence is repeated as many times as needed. With a single argument, that is exactly what we want, but it isn't necessarily with a sequence.

If we want that behavior, we can just use the named argument to Map, but if we want the function to be called with the entire sequence each time it is called, we must put the sequence as an argument to the MoreArgs parameter.

As an example, we can consider our trusted friend the scale function and make a version where a vector, x, is scaled by the mean and standard deviation of another vector, y:

```
scale <- function(x, y) (x - mean(y))/sd(y)
```

If we just provide Map with two arguments for scale, it will evaluate all pairs independently, and we will get a lot of NA values because we are calling the sd function on a single value:

```
unlist(Map(scale, 1:10, 1:5))
```

```
## [1] NA NA NA NA NA NA NA NA NA NA
```

The same happens if we name the parameter y:

```
unlist(Map(scale, 1:10, y = 1:5))
```

```
## [1] NA NA NA NA NA NA NA NA NA NA
```

but if we use MoreArgs, the entire vector y is provided to scale in each call:

```
unlist(Map(scale, 1:10, MoreArgs = list(y = 1:5)))
```

```
## [1] -1.2649111 -0.6324555  0.0000000  0.6324555
## [5]  1.2649111  1.8973666  2.5298221  3.1622777
## [9]  3.7947332  4.4271887
```

Just as `Filter`, `Map` can work with lists of arbitrary types as long as our function can handle the different types:

```
s <- list(a = 1:10, b = list(1,2,3,4,5,6),
          c = y ~ x1 + x2 + x3, d = vector("numeric"))
unlist(Map(length, s))
```

```
## a b c d
## 10 6 3 0
```

Reducing Sequences

While `Filter` and `Map` produces lists, the `Reduce` function transforms a list into a value. Of course, that value can also be a list—lists are also values—but `Reduce` doesn't simply process each element in its input list independently. Instead, it summarizes the list by applying a function iteratively to pairs. You provide it a function, `f`, of two elements, and it will first call `f` on the first two elements in the list. Then it will take the result of this and call `f` with this and the next element and continue doing that through the list.

So calling `Reduce(f, 1:5)` will be equivalent to calling

```
f(f(f(f(1, 2), 3), 4), 5)
```

It is just more readable to write `Reduce(f, 1:5)`, at least once you get used to it.

We can see it in action using `` `+` `` as the function:

```
Reduce(`+`, 1:5)
```

```
## [1] 15
```

You can also get stepwise results if you use the parameter `accumulate`. This will return a list of all the calls to f and include the first value in the list, so `Reduce(f, 1:5)` will return the list:

```
c(1, f(1, 2), f(f(1 ,2), 3), f(f(f(1, 2), 3), 4),
    f(f(f(f(1, 2), 3), 4), 5))
```

So, for addition, we get

```
Reduce(`+`, 1:5, accumulate = TRUE)
```

```
## [1]  1  3  6 10 15
```

By default, Reduce does its computations from left to right, but by setting the option `right` to TRUE, you instead get the results from right to left:

```
Reduce(`+`, 1:5, right = TRUE, accumulate = TRUE)
```

```
## [1] 15 14 12  9  5
```

For an associative operation like `+`, this will, of course, be the same result if we do not ask for the accumulative function calls.

In many functional programming languages, which all have this function (although it is sometimes called `fold` or `accumulate`), you need to provide an initial value for the computation. This is then used in the first call to f, so the folding instead starts with `f(init, x[1])` if init refers to the initial value and x is the sequence.

You can also get that behavior in R by explicitly giving Reduce an initial value through parameter `init`:

```
Reduce(`+`, 1:5, init = 10, accumulate = TRUE)
```

```
## [1] 10 11 13 16 20 25
```

You just don't need to specify this initial value that often. In languages that require it, it is used to get the right starting points when accumulating results. For addition, we would use zero as an initial value if we want Reduce to compute a sum because adding zero to the first value in the sequence would just get us the first element. For multiplication, we would instead have to use one as the initial value since that is how the first function application will just give us the initial value.

In R, we don't need to provide these initial values if we are happy with just having the first function call be on the first two elements in the list, so multiplication works just as well as addition without providing init:

```
Reduce(`*`, 1:5)
```

```
## [1] 120
```

```
Reduce(`*`, 1:5, accumulate = TRUE)
```

```
## [1]   1   2   6  24 120
```

```
Reduce(`*`, 1:5, right = TRUE, accumulate = TRUE)
```

```
## [1] 120 120  60  20   5
```

You wouldn't normally use Reduce for summarizing values as their sum or product, there are already functions in R for this (sum and prod, respectively), and these are much faster as they are low-level functions implemented in C, while Reduce has to be high level to handle arbitrary functions. For more complex data where we do not already have a function to summarize a list, Reduce is often the way to go.

Here is an example taken from Hadley Wickham's *Advanced R* book:

```
samples <- replicate(3, sample(1:10, replace = TRUE),
                                     simplify = FALSE)
str(samples)
```

```
## List of 3
```

```
## $ : int  [1:10] 1 3 7 8 9 5 9 1 6 4
## $ : int  [1:10] 4 5 8 3 1 6 9 10 5 3
## $ : int  [1:10] 9 9 2 10 9 2 9 8 7 10
```

```
Reduce(intersect, samples)
```

```
## [1] 8 9
```

We have a list of three vectors, each with ten samples of the numbers from one to ten, and we want to get the intersection of these three lists. That means taking the intersection of the first two and then taking the intersection of that result and the third list. Perfect for Reduce. We just combine it with the intersection function.

Bringing the Functions Together

The three functions are often used together, where Filter first gets rid of elements that should not be processed, then Map processes the list, and finally Reduce combines all the results.

This section will show a few examples of how we can use these functions together. We start with processing trees. Remember that we can construct trees using the make_node function we wrote earlier, and we can create a list of trees because we can create lists of anything:

```
A <- make_node("A")
C <- make_node("C", make_node("A"),
                    make_node("B"))
E <- make_node("E",
              make_node("C", make_node("A"), make_node("B")),
              make_node("D"))

trees <- list(A = A, C = C, E = E)
```

Printing a tree gives us the list representation of it. If we `unlist` a tree, we get the same representation, just flattened, so the structure is shown in the names of the resulting vector, but we wrote a `print_tree` function that gives us a string representation in Newick format:

```
trees[[2]]
```

```
## $name
## [1] "C"
##
## $left
## $left$name
## [1] "A"
##
## $left$left
## NULL
##
## $left$right
## NULL
##
##
## $right
## $right$name
## [1] "B"
##
## $right$left
## NULL
##
## $right$right
## NULL
```

```
unlist(trees[[2]])
```

```
##        name left.name right.name
##         "C"       "A"        "B"
```

```
print_tree(trees[[2]])
```

```
## [1] "(A,B)"
```

We can use `Map` to translate a list of trees into their Newick format and flatten this list to get a vector of characters:

```
Map(print_tree, trees)
```

```
## $A
## [1] "A"
##
## $C
## [1] "(A,B)"
##
## $E
## [1] "((A,B),D)"
```

```
unlist(Map(print_tree, trees))
```

```
##         A         C         E
##       "A"   "(A,B)" "((A,B),D)"
```

We can combine this with `Filter` to only get the trees that are not single leaves; here, we can use the `size_of_tree` function we wrote earlier:

```
unlist(Map(print_tree,
       Filter(function(tree) size_of_tree(tree) > 1,
       trees)))
```

```
##         C         E
##   "(A,B)" "((A,B),D)"
```

or we can get the size of all trees and compute their sum by combining Map with Reduce:

```
unlist(Map(size_of_tree, trees))
```

```
## A C E
## 1 3 5
```

```
Reduce(`+`, Map(size_of_tree, trees), 0)
```

```
## [1] 9
```

We can also search for the node depth of a specific node and, for example, get the depth of "B" in all the trees:

```
node_depth_B <- function(tree) node_depth(tree, "B")
unlist(Map(node_depth_B, trees))
```

```
##  A  C  E
## NA  1  2
```

The names we get in the result are just confusing. They refer to the names we gave the trees when we constructed the list, and we can get rid of them by using the parameter use.names in unlist. In general, if you don't need the names of a vector, you should always do this; it speeds up computations when R doesn't have to drag names along with the data you are working on.

```
unlist(Map(node_depth_B, trees), use.names = FALSE)
```

```
## [1] NA  1  2
```

For trees that do not have a "B" node, we get NA when we search for the node depth, and we can easily remove those using Filter:

```
Filter(function(x) !is.na(x),
       unlist(Map(node_depth_B, trees), use.names = FALSE))
```

```
## [1] 1 2
```

or we can explicitly check if a tree has node "B" before we Map over the trees:

```
has_B <- function(node) {
  if (node$name == "B") return(TRUE)
  if (is.null(node$left) && is.null(node$right)) return(FALSE)
  has_B(node$left) || has_B(node$right)
}
unlist(Map(node_depth_B, Filter(has_B, trees)), use.names = FALSE)
```

```
## [1] 1 2
```

The solution with filtering after mapping is probably preferable since we do not have to remember to match the has_B with node_depth_B if we replace them with general functions that handle arbitrary node names, but either solution will work.

The Apply Family of Functions

The Map function is a general solution for mapping over elements in a list, but R has a whole family of Map-like functions that operate on different types of input. These are all named "something"-apply, and we have already seen sapply in the previous chapter. The Map function is actually just a wrapper around one of these, the function mapply, and since we have already seen Map in use, I will not also discuss mapply, but I will give you a brief overview of the other functions in the apply family.

sapply, vapply, and lapply

The functions sapply, vapply, and lapply all operate on sequences. The difference is that sapply tries to *simplify* its output, vapply takes a value as an argument and will coerce its output to have the type of this value and give an error if it cannot, and lapply maps over lists.

Using sapply is convenient for interactive sessions since it essentially works like Map combined with unlist when the result of a map can be converted into a vector. Unlike unlist, it will not flatten a list, so if a map's result is more complex than a vector, sapply will still give you a list as its result. Because of this, sapply can be dangerous to use in a program. You don't necessarily know which type the output will have, so you have to program defensively and check if you get a vector or a list.

```
sapply(trees, size_of_tree)
```

```
## A C E
## 1 3 5
```

```
sapply(trees, identity)
```

```
##        A    C     E
## name   "A"  "C"   "E"
## left   NULL list,3 list,3
## right  NULL list,3 list,3
```

Using vapply, you get the same simplification as using sapply if the result can be transformed into a vector, but you have to tell the function what type the output should have. You do this by giving it an example of the desired output. If vapply cannot translate the result into that type, you get an error instead of a type of a different type, making the function safer to use in programs. After all, getting errors is better than unexpected results due to type confusion.

```
vapply(trees, size_of_tree, 1)
```

```
## A C E
## 1 3 5
```

The `lapply` is the function most similar to `Map`. It takes a list as input and returns a list. The main difference between `lapply` and `Map` is that `lapply` always operates on a *single* list, while `Map` can take multiple lists (which explains the name of `mapply`, the function that `Map` is a wrapper for).

```
lapply(trees, size_of_tree)
```

```
## $A
## [1] 1
##
## $C
## [1] 3
##
## $E
## [1] 5
```

The `apply` Function

The `apply` function works on matrices and higher-dimensional arrays instead of sequences. It takes three parameters plus any additional parameters that should just be passed along to the function called. The first parameter is the array to map over, the second is which dimension(s) we should marginalize along, and the third is the function we should apply.

We can see it in action by creating a matrix to apply over:

```
(m <- matrix(1:6, nrow=2, byrow=TRUE))
```

```
##      [,1] [,2] [,3]
## [1,]    1    2    3
## [2,]    4    5    6
```

To see what is actually happening, we will create a function that collects the data that it gets, so we can see exactly what it is called with:

```
collaps_input <- function(x) paste(x, collapse = ":")
```

If we marginalize on rows, it will be called on each of the two rows, and the function will be called with the entire row vectors:

```
apply(m, 1, collaps_input)
## [1] "1:2:3" "4:5:6"
```

If we marginalize on columns, it will be called on each of the three columns and produce tree strings:

```
apply(m, 2, collaps_input)
## [1] "1:4" "2:5" "3:6"
```

If we marginalize on both rows and columns, it will be called on every single element instead:

```
apply(m, c(1, 2), collaps input)
##      [,1] [,2] [,3]
## [1,] "1"  "2"  "3"
## [2,] "4"  "5"  "6"
```

The `tapply` Function

The `tapply` function works on so-called ragged tables: tables where the rows can have different lengths. You cannot directly make an array with different sizes of dimensions in rows, but you can use a flat vector combined with factors that indicate which virtual dimensions you are using. The `tapply` function groups the vector according to a factor and then calls its function with each group:

```
(x <- rnorm(10))
```

```
##  [1]  1.58827631 -0.99044548 -1.56081835
##  [4]  0.38316964  1.82773685 -0.96031940
##  [7] -1.32439441  0.09413377 -0.02306317
## [10] -0.60627476
```

```
(categories <- sample(c("A", "B", "C"), size = 10, replace
= TRUE))
```

```
## [1] "A" "A" "A" "B" "C" "A" "B" "A" "C" "A"
```

```
tapply(x, categories, mean)
```

```
##           A           B           C
## -0.4059080 - 0.4706124  0.9023368
```

You can use more than one factor if you wrap the factors in a list:

```
(categories2 <- sample(c("X", "Y"), size = 10, replace = TRUE))
```

```
##  [1] "X" "Y" "X" "Y" "Y" "X" "X" "Y" "Y" "X"
```

```
tapply(x, list(categories, categories2), mean)
```

```
##            X          Y
## A -0.384784 -0.4481559
## B -1.324394  0.3831696
## C        NA  0.9023368
```

Functional Programming in `purrr`

The `Filter`, `Map`, and `Reduce` functions are the building blocks of many functional algorithms. However, many common operations require various combinations of the three functions, and combinations with `unlist`, so writing functions using *only* these three/four functions means building functions from the most basic building blocks. This is inefficient, so you want a toolbox of more specific functions for common operations.

The package purrr implements a number of such functions for more effective functional programming and also provides its own versions of Filter, Map, and Reduce. A complete coverage of the purrr package is beyond the scope of this short book, but I will give a quick overview of the functions available in the package and urge you to explore the package more if you are serious about using functional programming in R.

```
library(purrr)
```

The functions in purrr all take the sequence they operate on as their first argument—similar to the apply family of functions but different from the Filter, Map, and Reduce functions.

Filter-like Functions

The purrr analog of Filter is called keep and works exactly like Filter. It takes a predicate and returns a list of the elements in a sequence where the predicate returns TRUE. The function discard works similarly but returns the elements where the predicate returns FALSE:

```
keep(1:5, \(x) x > 3)
```

```
## [1] 4 5
```

```
discard(1:5, \(x) x > 3)
```

```
## [1] 1 2 3
```

If you give these functions a vector, you get a vector back, of the same type, and if you give them a list, you will get a list back:

```
keep(as.list(1:5), \(x) x > 3)
```

```
## [[1]]
## [1] 4
##
## [[2]]
## [1] 5
```

Two convenience functions that you could implement by checking the length of the list returned by Filter are every and some that check if all elements in the sequence satisfy the predicate or if some elements satisfy the predicate:

```
every(1:5, \(x) x > 0)
```

```
## [1] TRUE
```

```
every(1:5, \(x) x > 3)
```

```
## [1] FALSE
```

```
some(1:5, \(x) x > 3)
```

```
## [1] TRUE
```

```
some(1:5, \(x) x > 6)
```

```
## [1] FALSE
```

In the examples here, I have used the \(x) ... syntax introduced in R 4, but with purrr, developed before we had this syntax, you can also use formulae to define short functions. You can use the "formula notation" and define an anonymous function by writing ˜ followed by the body of the function, where the function argument is referred to by the variable .x:

```
keep(1:5, ˜ .x > 3)
```

```
## [1] 4 5
```

```
discard(1:5, ~ .x > 3)
```

```
## [1] 1 2 3
```

This shorthand for anonymous functions is only available within functions from purrr, though. Just because you have imported the purrr package, you will not get the functionality in other functions.

Map-like Functions

The Map functionality comes in different flavors in purrr, depending on the type of output you want and the number of input sequences you need to map over.

The map function always returns a list, while functions map_lgl, map_int, map_dbl, and map_chr return vectors of logical values, integer values, numeric (double) values, and characters, respectively.

```
map(1:5, ~ .x + 2)
```

```
## [[1]]
## [1] 3
##
## [[2]]
## [1] 4
##
## [[3]]
## [1] 5
##
## [[4]]
## [1] 6
##
## [[5]]
## [1] 7
```

141

```
map_dbl(1:5, ~ .x + 2)
```

```
## [1] 3 4 5 6 7
```

The map family of functions all take a single sequence as input, but there are corresponding functions for two sequences, the map2 family, and for an arbitrary number of sequences, the pmap family.

For the map2 functions, you can create anonymous functions that refer to the two input values they will be called with by using variables .x and .y:

```
map2(1:5, 6:10, ~ 2 * .x + .y)
```

```
## [[1]]
## [1] 8
##
## [[2]]
## [1] 11
##
## [[3]]
## [1] 14
##
## [[4]]
## [1] 17
##
## [[5]]
## [1] 20
```

```
map2_dbl(1:5, 6:10, ~ 2 * .x + .y)
```

```
## [1]  8 11 14 17 20
```

142

For arbitrary numbers of sequences, you must use the pmap family and wrap the sequences in a list that is given as the first parameter. If you use anonymous functions, you will need to define them using the general R syntax; there are no shortcuts for specifying anonymous functions with three or more parameters.

```
pmap(list(1:5, 6:10, 11:15), \(x, y, z) x + y + z)
```

```
## [[1]]
## [1] 18
##
## [[2]]
## [1] 21
##
## [[3]]
## [1] 24
##
## [[4]]
## [1] 27
##
## [[5]]
## [1] 30
```

```
pmap_dbl(list(1:5, 6:10, 11:15), \(x, y, z) x + y + z)
```

```
## [1] 18 21 24 27 30
```

The function map_if provides a variation of map that only applies the function it is mapping if a predicate is TRUE. If the predicate returns FALSE for an element, that element is kept unchanged.

For example, we can use it to multiply only numbers that are not even by two like this:

```
unlist(map_if(1:5, ~ .x %% 2 == 1, ~ 2*.x))
```

```
## [1]  2  2  6  4 10
```

A particularly nice feature of purrr's map functions is that you can provide them with a string instead of a function, and this is used when you are working with sequences of elements that have names, like data frames and lists, to extract named components. So if we map over the trees from earlier, we can, for example, use map to extract the left child of all the trees:

```
map_chr(map(keep(trees, ~ size_of_tree(.x) > 1), "left"),
        print_tree)
```

```
##         C        E
##       "A" "(A,B)"
```

Here, we combine three different functions: we use keep so we only look at trees that actually *have* a left child. Then we use map with "left" to extract the left child, and, finally, we use map_chr to translate the trees into Newick format for printing.

Reduce-like Functions

The Reduce function is implemented in the reduce function:

```
reduce(1:5, `+`)
```

```
## [1] 15
```

```
reduce(1:5, `*`, .dir = "backward") # Reduce from the right
```

```
## [1] 120
```

CHAPTER 7

Point-Free Programming

In this last chapter, we will not so much discuss actual programming but a programming style called *point-free programming* (not *pointless* programming), which is characterized by constructing functions through a composition of other functions rather than writing new functions.

A lot of computing can be expressed as the steps that data flow through and how data is transformed along the way. We write functions to handle all the most basic steps, the atoms of a program, and then construct functions for more complex operations by combining more fundamental transformations, building program molecules from the program atoms.

The term *point-free* refers to the intermediate states data can be in when computing a sequence of transformations. The *points* it refers to are the states the data is in after each transformation, and *point-free* means that we do not focus on these points in any way. They are simply not mentioned anywhere in code written using point-free programming.

This might all sound a bit abstract, but if you are used to writing pipelines in shell scripts, it should soon become very familiar because point-free programming is exactly what you do when you write a pipeline. There, data flow through a number of programs tied together. The output of one program becomes the input for the next in the pipeline, and you never refer to the intermediate data, only the steps of transformations the data go through as the pipeline processes it.

© Thomas Mailund 2023
T. Mailund, *Functional Programming in R 4*, https://doi.org/10.1007/978-1-4842-9487-1_7

Function Composition

The simplest way to construct new functions from more basic ones is through function composition. In mathematics, if we have a function, f, mapping from domain A to domain B, which we can write as $f: A \rightarrow B$, and another function g, $g: A \rightarrow C$, we can create a new function $h: A \rightarrow C$ by composing the two: $h(x) = g(f(x))$.

We can do exactly the same thing in R and define h in terms of functions f and g like this:

```
h <- function(x) g(f(x))
```

There is a lot of extra fluff in writing a new function explicitly just to combine two other functions. In mathematical notation, we don't write the combination of two functions that way. We write the function composition as $h = g \circ f$. Composing functions to define new functions, rather than defining functions that just explicitly call others, is what we call point-free programming, and it is easily done in R.

You can write a composition function, a higher-order function that takes two functions as arguments and returns their composition:

```
compose <- function(g, f) function(...) g(f(...))
```

We can then use this function to handle a common case when we are using Map and frequently want to unlist the result. We could use Map and then unlist by explicitly calling them, of course:

```
xs <- 1:4
unlist(Map(\(x) x + 2, xs)) # explicit Map + unlist call

## [1] 3 4 5 6
```

but we could also compose Map and unlist to create a new mapping function from their composition:

```
umap <- compose(unlist, Map) # composing Map and unlist
umap(\(x) x + 2, xs)         # using the new function
```

```
## [1] 3 4 5 6
```

To get something similar to the mathematical notation, we want it to be an infix operator, but the package pryr has already defined it for us so we can write the same code as this:

```
library(pryr)
umap <- unlist %.% Map
umap(\(x) x + 2, xs)
```

```
## [1] 3 4 5 6
```

We are not limited to only composing two functions, and since function composition is associative, we don't need to worry about the order in which they are composed, so we don't need to use parentheses around compositions. We can combine three or more functions as well, and we can combine functions with anonymous functions if we need some extra functionality that isn't already implemented as a named function. For example, we could define a function for computing the root mean square error like this:

```
rmse <- sqrt %.% mean %.% \(x, y) (x - y)**2
rmse(1:4, 2:5)
```

```
## [1] 1
```

We need a new function for computing the squared distance between x and y, so we add an anonymous function for that, but then we can just use mean and sqrt to get the rest of the functionality.

In the mathematical notation for function composition, you always write the functions you compose in the same order as you would write them if you explicitly called them, so $h°g°f$ would be evaluated on a value x as $h(g(f(x)))$. This is great if you are used to reading from right to left, but if you are used to reading left to right, it is a bit backward.

Of course, nothing prevents us from writing a function composition operator that reverses the order of the functions. To avoid confusion with the mathematical notation for function composition, we would use a different operator so we could define ; such that $f; g = g°f$ and in R use that for function composition:

```
`%;%` <- function(f, g) function(...) g(f(...))
rmse <- (\(x, y) (x - y)**2) %;% mean %;% sqrt
rmse(1:4, 2:5)
```

```
## [1] 1
```

Here, I need parentheses around the anonymous function to prevent R from considering the composition as part of the function body, but otherwise, the functionality is the same as before; we can just read the composition from left to right.

Pipelines

The magrittr package introduced a "left-to-right" function composition as the operator %>%, and with R 4.1 we got a built-in operator |> with the same purpose. Although they differ slightly in syntax and flexibility, both aim at making data analysis pipelines easier to read and write by specifying transformations in a left-to-right pipeline syntax. Both allow you to chain together various data transformations and analyses in ways very similar to how you chain together command-line tools in shell pipelines. The various

operations are function calls, and these functions are chained together
with the %>% or |> operators, moving the output of one function to the
input of the next.

For example, to take the vector 1:4, get the mean of it, and then take the
sqrt, you can write a pipeline like this:

```
library(magrittr)
1:4 %>% mean %>% sqrt
```

```
## [1] 1.581139
```

or using |>:

```
1:4 |> mean() |> sqrt()
```

```
## [1] 1.581139
```

When using %>%, you can compose functions by their names, mean %>%
sqrt, but with |> you have to compose function calls mean() |> sqrt().
The %>% operator also accesses the latter syntax.

The default is that the output from the previous step in the pipeline
is passed as the first argument to the next function in the pipeline. To
write your own functions to fit into this pattern, you just need to make the
data that come through a pipeline the first argument for your function.
Because pipelines are now frequently used in R, this is the pattern that
most functions follow, and it is used in popular packages like dplyr and
tidyr. The purrr package is also designed to work well with magrittr
pipelines. All its functions take the data they operate on as their first
parameter, so stringing together several transformations using %>% or |> is
straightforward.

Not all functions follow the pattern, mostly older functions do not, but
you can use the variable "." to refer to the data being passed along the
pipeline when you need it to go at a different position than the first:

```
data.frame(x = 1:4, y = 2:5) %>% plot(y ~ x, data = .)
```

This is only supported by the %>% operator and not |>, though.

If the input is a data frame, you can access its columns using the column names as you would with any other data frame. The argument is still "." and you just need to use that parameter to refer to the data:

```
data.frame(x = 1:4, y = 2:5) %>% plot(.$x, .$y)
```

The "." parameter can be used several times in a function call in the pipeline and can be used together with function calls in a pipeline, for example:

```
rnorm(4) %>% data.frame(x = ., y = cos(.))
```

```
##             x            y
## 1 -0.4606873   0.89574717
## 2 -0.2682750   0.96422956
## 3 -0.5016734   0.87677906
## 4 -1.6209375  -0.05012016
```

There is one caveat: if "." *only* appears in function calls, it will *also* be given to the function as a first parameter. This means that code such as the following example will create a data frame with three variables, the first being a column named ".":

```
rnorm(4) %>% data.frame(x = sin(.), y = cos(.))
```

```
##             .            x           y
## 1   0.78527169   0.70701735  0.7071962
## 2  -0.01757641  -0.01757551  0.9998455
## 3  -0.24785011  -0.24532033  0.9694421
## 4  -0.37395301  -0.36529810  0.9308906
```

While the %>% operator is mainly intended for writing such data processing pipelines, it can also be used for defining new functions by composing other functions, this time with the functions written in left-to-right order. You write such functions just as you would write data processing pipelines, but let the first step in the pipeline be "." so this is a data pipeline:

```
mean_sqrt <- 1:4 %>% mean %>% sqrt
mean_sqrt
```

```
## [1] 1.581139
```

while this is a function:

```
mean_sqrt <- . %>% mean %>% sqrt
mean_sqrt(1:4)
```

```
## [1] 1.581139
```

and you can use this function in a pipeline:

```
1:4 %>% mean_sqrt
```

```
## [1] 1.581139
```

The |> operator does not support this kind of writing functions; you can use it to compose function calls, but it is only syntactic sugar for calling functions, not for defining them. When it comes to defining functions, the %>% operator is more flexible.

You can only use this approach to define functions taking a single argument as input. If you need more than one argument, you will need to define your function explicitly. The whole pipeline pattern works by assuming that it is a single piece of data that is passed along between function calls. Still, nothing prevents you from having complex data, such as data frames, and emulating having more than one argument in this way.

Take, for example, the root mean square error function we wrote earlier:

```
rmse <- (\(x, y) (x - y)**2) %;% mean %;% sqrt
```

This function takes two arguments, so we cannot create it using ".". We can instead change it to take a single argument, for example, a data frame, and get the two values from there:

```
rmse <- . %>% { (.$x - .$y)**2 } %>% mean %>% sqrt
data.frame(x = 1:4, y = 2:5) %>% rmse
```

```
## [1] 1
```

Here, we also used another feature of magrittr, a less verbose syntax for writing anonymous functions. By writing the expression {(.$x - .$y)**2} in curly braces, we are making a function in which we can refer to the argument as ".".

Being able to write anonymous functions by just putting expressions in braces is very convenient when the data needs to be massaged just a little to fit the output of one function to the expected input of the next.

Anonymous functions also prevent the "." parameter from getting implicitly passed as the first argument to a function when it is otherwise only used in function calls. If the expression is wrapped in curly braces, then the function call is not modified in any way, and so "." is not implicitly added as a first parameter:

```
rnorm(4) %>% { data.frame(x = sin(.), y = cos(.)) }
```

```
##            x          y
## 1  0.5526906  0.8333865
## 2 -0.8979247  0.4401492
## 3 -0.9402584 -0.3404616
## 4  0.4508160  0.8926169
```

CHAPTER 8

Conclusions

This concludes this book on functional programming in R. You now know all the basic programming patterns used in day-to-day functional programming and how to use them in the R programming language.

Getting used to writing functional programs might take a little effort if you are only used to imperative or object-oriented programming, but the combination of higher-order functions and closures is a very powerful paradigm for effective programming, and writing pure functions whenever possible makes for code that is much simpler to reason about.

R is not a pure functional programming language, though, so your code will usually mix imperative programming—which in most cases means using loops instead of recursions, both for convenience and efficiency reasons—with functional patterns. With careful programming, you can still keep the changing states of a program to a minimum and keep most of your program pure.

Helping you keep programming pure is the immutability of data in R. Whenever you "modify" data, you will implicitly create a copy of the data and then modify the copy. For reasoning about your programs, that is good news. It is very hard to create side effects of functions. It does come with some drawbacks, however. Many classical data structures assume that you can modify data. Since you cannot do this in R, you will instead have to construct your data structures such that updating them means creating new, modified, data structures.

© Thomas Mailund 2023
T. Mailund, *Functional Programming in R 4*, https://doi.org/10.1007/978-1-4842-9487-1_8

We have seen how we can use linked lists ("next lists" in the terminology I have used in this book) and trees with functions that modify the data when computing on it. Lists and trees form the basic constructions for data structures in functional programs, but efficient functional data structures are beyond the scope of this book. I plan to return to it in a later book in the series.

I will end the book here, but I hope it is not the end of your exploration of functional programming in R.

Index

A

apply function, 136
as.list function, 121

B

baseenv() function, 73

C

Closures, 84–86
Continuation-passing style, 105–112
counter function, 87, 89
Curried function, 98
curry function, 102, 103

D

Data structures, 7, 26, 51, 120,
153, 154
depth_first_numbers function, 89
do.call function, 101
Dynamic scope, 90, 91

E

environment() function, 69, 78
environment(f), 78, 79
eval() function, 66, 67

F

Filter function, 119, 120, 122–124,
127, 132, 133, 138–141
formals function, 100
Functional Programming, 1, 100,
139, 145, 153

G

Global environment, 66, 69, 70
Global scope, 14, 15, 18, 66
Global variables, 5, 41, 68, 70

H

Higher-order functions, 93

I, J, K

Infix operators
arithmetic operators, 28
control structures, 29
match.call function, 30
replicate function, 29
R/even control
structures, 28
user-defined, 27
operator %x%, 29

© Thomas Mailund 2023
T. Mailund, *Functional Programming in R 4*, https://doi.org/10.1007/978-1-4842-9487-1

Printed in the United States
by Baker & Taylor Publisher Services